FLEA MARKET
FINDS
& HOW TO RESTORE THEM

FLEA MARKET FINDS
& HOW TO RESTORE THEM

CAROLINE ATKINS

COLLINS & BROWN

First published in Great Britain in 2002
by Collins & Brown Limited
64 Brewery Road
London N7 9NT

www.chrysalisbooks.co.uk

A member of **Chrysalis** Books plc

Distributed in the United States and Canada
by Sterling Publishing Co.
387 Park Avenue South, New York, NY 10016 USA

Published in association with The National Magazine Company
Limited.

9 8 7 6 5 4 3 2 1

British Library Cataloguing-in-Publication Data:
A catalogue record for this book is available from the British
Library.

ISBN 1 85585 960 2

Editor: Gillian Haslam
Copy Editor: Alison Wormleighton
Designer: Christine Wood

Reproduction by Alliance Graphics Ltd, UK
Printed and bound by Craft Print International Ltd, Singapore
This book was typeset using Bembo and Futura

contents

introduction

The pleasure of flea market browsing is two parts curiosity to one part anticipation – the enjoyment of free-range rummaging laced with the excitement of knowing that, every now and then, you'll come across buried treasure. It may be something you've been searching for – the missing cup or plate that completes the set; a bedroom quilt in just the right colours – or you may simply fall unexpectedly in love with a faded picture, a comfortable old chair or the way the light glows through a collection of coloured glass bottles. This book provides practical answers to the questions you'll have about the objects you find, with advice on the checks to make before you buy, and the care and cleaning routines to follow afterwards.

Each chapter in the book covers a different material, from glass, ceramics and metal to textiles, leather and wood. Many items will have a personal appeal that makes them worth your price even if no one else wants them, and occasionally you may come across bargains that have more value than the seller realised. Often, though, you'll find that the more sought-after collectables have already been picked out by dealers and are now commanding serious collectors' prices in specialist shops and antique markets. Until you become practised at spotting things of interest and getting a feel for their age, origin and possible value, you'll probably make mistakes – paying more than is sensible for damaged items or reproduction novelties, while missing gems that would be worth snapping up. The learning process is part of the fun, and gradually you will build up knowledge and confidence. So enjoy the browsing for its own sake and, when you buy, make sure it's because you really like something, not just because you think it's an investment.

Whatever you end up taking home with you, treat it with respect. This book collects together traditional techniques and expert advice for cleaning, restoring and using flea market finds, but opinions often differ, so you may need to try several suggestions before you find the one you feel most comfortable with. Always test an inconspicuous area before tackling the larger object, and always play safe if you suspect the item may be old or valuable. Attempts to repair or restore it yourself may do irreparable damage, so take it to a conservation expert or professional restorer (there's a list of useful contacts on pages 148–156) and follow their advice for keeping your find safe and well cared for in future.

hints for buying from markets

❍ Arrive at markets as early as you possibly can. Professional dealers will have a shrewd eye for the best bargains, so you need to be there at the start of trading to have any chance of competing with them.

❍ Take your time and check for damage and restoration work – you may spot something the dealer has missed, and use it to negotiate the price down.

❍ Always look past superficial damage – a good shape and basically sound condition can easily be transformed with a little attention.

❍ For a better deal, buy several items from one dealer and suggest a lower overall price.

❍ Have plenty of cash with you – most dealers won't accept charge or credit cards, and cash will be more appealing than cheques.

❍ Don't treat the market like a Middle Eastern souk – ask for the best price, but don't expect massive reductions. If you like a piece, be prepared to pay for it.

❍ Familiarize yourself with a particular market before you start buying. Get a feel for the goods and their prices so that you know what things are likely to cost.

❍ Get to know individual traders who can pass on their expertise and start to look out for pieces you'll like.

❍ Ask if you can leave your purchases behind the stall to collect later – or have large pieces delivered to your door for a small fee.

❍ Be careful with old electrical goods – the cost involved in making them work again may not be worth the effort, and they may not comply with today's strict electrical safety regulations. It may be better to buy them simply for decorative purposes.

textiles

Old textiles have the past woven into their threads – the hands that stitched them, the people who wore them, the rooms in which they were used. It's a very personal history, enriched with everyday wear and touched by domestic detail. The fabrics we discover in forgotten cupboards and on flea market stalls are all part of the story – not only the carefully worked schoolroom samplers and decorative embroidery, but the practical pieces too. There are the bedcovers, tablecloths and kitchen linens that served households before our own, and the patchwork quilts that used up spare fragments rather than letting them go to waste.

Some pieces have historical or sentimental value – hand-stitched tapestries and christening gowns, for example. These should be looked after with care and taken to professional restorers if necessary. But domestic and dress fabrics belong to a tradition of recycling: clothes have been cut down and remade; linens trimmed and reworked when they wore thin. The best compliment you can pay them is to continue that tradition by putting your finds to good use.

Q I've found a beautiful patchwork quilt – a cottage-style affair incorporating dozens of different fabrics. Some of these have worn less well than others, so that a few of the patches are now starting to fray. Can I replace individual sections?

A There's a wonderful sense of history about handmade patchworks – even modern ones – because of the way they immortalize elements of the maker's world. The snippets of fabrics left over from dressmaking and furnishings, the scraps of paper and card cut up to make the templates: all these are worked into the quilt in a kind of domestic collage. Some of the fabrics may be classics such as gingham, ticking or candy stripes, and these can be replaced without too much difficulty – but where other patches are torn or frayed, you probably won't be able to match the pattern precisely. The key thing is to find fabrics of the same weight so that they don't pull or tear each other. Ideally they should also be of the same period. Therefore, if you think your quilt has any historical value, it's best to check with a professional restorer before attempting a repair.

Quilts were made to be used, not displayed, so if you want to contribute to this corner of domestic history, add your own fabrics to the mix and let it evolve for a new generation to enjoy. Cut out the damaged piece by snipping the stitching around it very carefully with small, sharp, pointed sewing scissors. If there is quilting across the patch, cut through the quilting stitches, too, from the top of the quilt. Remove the patch so that you're left with a hole in the patchwork (but not in the filling or backing). Cut a new piece of fabric (which has been pre-shrunk if you intend ever to wash the quilt) and slip it inside this hole so that the edges are concealed. Slipstitch it neatly in place. Replace any quilting stitches by hand, matching the quilting on the rest of the quilt.

To prevent further damage to the fabric, try to keep the quilt away from strong sunlight, which causes fading and sun rot, and dry-clean rather than washing it. If the worst comes to the worst and you find that parts of the quilt are beyond repair, don't give up on the whole thing: cut out sound sections to turn into cushions or to frame and hang on the wall.

Right: Old quilts can be mended and individual patches replaced if they have worn or frayed.

Q I've chanced on a pair of old linen curtains that are the perfect length for one of my windows, but the bottom edges are badly worn in places. What's the best way of mending or disguising them?

A Moths, sunlight and general wear may all take their toll on curtain fabric, especially along the bottom edges, where long curtains can drag on the floor, and along the inner vertical edges, which are constantly being handled. The simplest way to repair this sort of wear is to trim the curtains with borders of new fabric. It should preferably contrast with the original fabric, as this will give the curtains a definite finish rather than looking like a patch-up job.

For a softer, more old-fashioned effect, try the technique used by the British designer John Fowler, who created a set of curtains with a scalloped flounce down the inner edges and along the bottom for the drawing room of a restored 17th-century London house. Inspired by a set of 19th-century hangings in a Dutch castle, the improvised frill was made from individual patches or 'petals' of fabric cut with pinking shears and stitched to the curtain edges. The technique works best with faded, country-house-style fabrics.

Q I'm an incurable collector of old clothes from flea markets. Even if the garment isn't my size or style, I fall in love with the fabrics and hoard them without being able to think of a practical use for them. Any ideas?

A The problem with clothing is that the amount of fabric each item provides is relatively small, with seams, darts, pockets and so on generally getting in the way. If you have a lot of clothing to choose from, the best way to make the most of it is to cut the usable parts into smallish squares and then mix the different fabrics in new combinations to create a patchwork. You may not have enough to make a whole quilt, but cushions won't need nearly as many patches. And because of their smaller scale, they allow you to experiment with radical mixes and flamboyant colours that you probably wouldn't dare use for larger items.

Even old knitted jerseys can be recycled in this way, if you machine-wash them on a hot cycle first. This makes the wool shrink to create a firmer, felted fabric that is easier to work with and less likely to unravel.

To make a patchwork knitted cushion

1 Cut the washed knitwear into squares: you want 16 squares (four rows of four) to make the cushion front, so first measure your cushion pad and then cut the squares so that they will cover this size when overlapped by 1cm (⅜in). You will also need to allow for a 1cm (⅜in) seam allowance around the outer edges of the cushion front.

2 Lay the squares out in a patchwork, overlapping the edges by 1cm (⅜in). This creates a simpler, more rustic effect than the more usual method of turning under the seam allowances. Topstitch the pieces together, taking care not to stretch them.

3 Cut a cushion back from cotton, linen or corduroy, the same size as the cushion front. Stitch the front and back together around three edges, with right sides together and taking a 1cm (⅜in) seam. Turn the cover right side out, turn under the fourth edge neatly and attach ties (made from corduroy or felt strips) to fasten.

Right: Old knitwear, hot-washed to 'felt' the wool, can be cut into patchwork pieces and recycled as a cushion cover.

---

collecting scraps

It's worth looking out for any materials that would be suitable for recycling into patchworks, cushion covers and accessories such as lavender or pot-pourri bags, herb pillows, hot-water-bottle covers, pincushions and covered coat-hangers. You won't need large quantities of fabric for these, so second-hand summer dresses and men's shirts are among the best sources of useful cottons, providing a stock of bright colours and interesting patterns from which you can select pieces for different projects.

Q How can I create textile panels to line the front of an old wardrobe?

A Sometimes the solid wood of wardrobe doors makes the furniture look just too heavy and dominant for a bedroom. Replacing the central panels with fabric creates a much lighter effect, so this is a great way of using up old curtain material and bedcovers acquired at flea markets. With the wood of the door providing a strong supporting frame, the fabric won't be subject to much wear, and if you gather it, worn or faded patches will be less noticeable.

You need the right style of wardrobe to make the most of this effect: the panels need to be easily removable, so that you don't have to dismantle the whole front. Don't wreck a beautiful wardrobe just for the sake of a change, but if the front is damaged or rickety, use this as a way to repair it. Drill a large hole through the centre of the panel, then cut the bulk of it away with an electric jigsaw. Now pull the remaining pieces out of the slots that hold them in place around the edges.

This is also a good solution if the door is fitted with a mirror whose silvering is past its best, as fabric can be used to replace the mirror, with the shape of the opening creating an interesting frame. How you remove the mirror depends on the construction of the wardrobe, but you should be able to prise away the panel behind the mirror, then remove the blocks holding it in place.

You can use the fabric flat or gathered. If it is in good condition, it can be stretched over a sheet of hardboard. Cut the board to a slightly larger size than the space it is to fill, making sure it will still fit through the door to be positioned in place. Lay the fabric over it, positioning any motifs carefully, and staple or glue the edges behind. Because the door panel will be visible when the wardrobe is open, you may want to cover both sides with fabric. For a more decorative effect, or if the fabric is less hard-wearing, attach curtain

Left: Replacing wardrobe doors with gathered panels of fabric creates a softer, prettier effect then solid wood.

wire inside the door at top and bottom, then stitch narrow channels at the top and bottom of the fabric so it can be threaded onto the wires and gathered into folds.

Q I love the old-fashioned stitching and stripes of traditional woollen blankets. I bought a batch second-hand, but my family prefers duvets. How else can I use them?

A Traditional blankets provide bands of striping and neatly stitched edges that are perfect for reconstructing into cushion covers and soft, fleecy pillowcases. For an old-fashioned fabric, these designs have a surprisingly contemporary style, which adds to their impact. This is a good way to make use of areas of sound fabric in blankets that have been damaged by moths or scorch marks. And because the pattern is the same on both sides, you can use whichever side is in better condition.

The simplest way is to cut your cushion or pillow shape so it follows the striped patterning – for example, by positioning a band of stripes across the centre. Stitch the front to the back piece, right sides together, around three edges, then turn the cover right side out and finish the fourth edge with a zipper. If you wish, blanket-stitch around the edges to recreate the original blanket effect.

You can even make use of the original stitching. Instead of making the front from one complete panel, cut two smaller pieces, using the stitched edge of the blanket for one of these. This piece should be half the depth of the cushion, and the other piece about 5cm (2in) deeper than that. Cut out one square for the back. With right sides together, lay the smaller front piece on the top half of the back piece, so the stitched edge runs across the middle. Lay the other piece over the bottom half, again with right sides together, and turning a hem towards you to finish the edge. Pin the edges and across the centre, then machine stitch around all four edges. When you turn it right side out, the blanket stitching will run in a neat line across the front, concealing the opening which can be finished with buttons or press studs (snaps).

Q I've bought a set of dining chairs with drop-in seats covered in very worn fabric. The chairs themselves are in good condition and the seats are well padded. Can I just replace the fabric?

A Yes, very easily. You're lucky that the padding is still firm, as replacing this would have involved more work (and felt more like serious upholstery than a quick repair). As it is, the simple design of the drop-in seats means this is the most basic kind of furniture rescue, with no special skills needed.

To cover a drop-in seat

1 First remove the seat by pushing it up from beneath (or, if it's more firmly wedged, turn the chair upside down and knock it gently around the edges with a hammer wrapped in a cloth). Now pull out the nails or staples attaching the existing fabric to the wooden seat frame and pull the fabric away.

2 If your luck continues to hold, there may be a calico (muslin) lining beneath. If not, it's a good idea to add your own, as this will help protect your new seat covers from wearing out as fast as the old ones. Cut a panel of calico (muslin) that will fit over the top and sides of the seat and overlap underneath by around 6cm (2¼in). Stretch it tight, folding the fabric neatly into the corners. Using a staple gun, staple the edges into place along the underside of the frame.

3 Repeat the process with your top fabric, cutting it slightly larger this time so that you have enough to turn under the edges for a neat finish.

Q Traditional embroidered tray cloths and dressing table runners are very pretty but not terribly practical these days. How else could I use the fabric?

A Linens like these provide panels of hemmed, edged and decorated cloth, perfect for recycling as pillow or cushion covers, or for hanging as simple curtains. To turn them into

cushion covers, simply back the embroidered cloth with contrasting cotton fabric – ginghams, stripes, florals or paisleys, or solid colours that accent the embroidery. Curtains are even easier to make. Think of the simple panels you often see hanging in the windows of continental village houses – one at each small casement, threaded onto a slim wire or pole across the top. Either turn a 3cm (1¼in) hem at the top of the fabric to create a basic casing, or attach a strip of 3cm- (1¼in-) wide plain tape or ribbon across the top, stitching along both edges of the tape, to create a channel that can be slotted onto the pole.

Q I've bought myself a whole stack of traditional kitchen linens – tablecloths, napkins and tea towels – which I couldn't resist because they were in such good condition. There are far more than I'll ever need. How else can I make use of them?

A The beauty of traditional kitchen linens is their simplicity. The colours are usually

practical primaries on a white background; the patterning, plain stripes and plaids, sometimes with more delicate designs worked into the wider bands of the weave.

The handy sizes of tea towels and napkins make them perfect for recycling as laundry bags, shoe bags and pyjama cases. Just stitch two together around three edges and make a casing along the open neck for a drawstring to be threaded through. Or fold a single tea towel into an envelope shape, stitch the two side edges and then add a button fastening to the front opening.

One of the most effective ways of using old linens is to pick a colour theme and then stitch together different pieces of matching shades to create slipcovers for comfortable armchairs. The key to making a success of this is to select the right fabric pieces for each part of the chair, so that elements of the design follow its lines and accent the shape.

To make a chair slipcover

1 If the chair already has an old slipcover, you could cut the pieces apart to make a pattern.

Otherwise, cut a paper pattern to fit the chair, treating each part of it as a separate section – the seat, the back, over the arms from the seat down to the floor, the front of the arms and the front of the seat. Add 2.5cm (1in) to all edges for seam allowances and minor adjustments.

2 Now sort out your linens to find sections of fabric that fit the various pattern pieces, thinking about where these will be positioned on the chair and how any design elements will fall. Once you've got your basic shape, you can be more flexible with the pieces – perhaps using a single piece for the seat and front if that seems to fit the fabric better, or a single piece folded over the back of the chair instead of separate pieces.

3 Pin the pieces together, and try the cover on the chair to check that it fits. Make any necessary adjustments, then stitch, with right sides together. Trim the seam allowances and turn the slipcover right side out.

Below: Traditional kitchen linens and tablecloths can be stitched together to make loose chair covers.

LOOKING AFTER LACE

Keep unused lace well protected until you find a home for it. Wash it in tepid water and soapflakes and store in dark, dry conditions, preferably wrapped in acid-free paper (see pages 148-156). Be careful, though, about cleaning lace that has been coloured with tea or coffee. The Victorians often dipped lace to age it – and also to hide marks – so if you remove the colouring you may simply end up with a set of original antique stains. If washing leaves your lace limp and floppy, you can stiffen it by dipping it in a solution made from 25g (1oz) gum arabic in 250ml (1 cup) of boiling water. Wait until the solution is cool, then dip the lace, leave it to dry, and finally press with a cool iron through a muslin cloth.

Q I have collected old lace for years. Some of it is quite delicate and has to be kept for display only, but I have lots of more robust, less precious pieces that I'd love to use somehow. Have you any ideas that won't look too frilly or Victorian?

A Lace is so pretty and intricately worked that small quantities are all that is needed to add a touch of old-fashioned romance to your furnishings: too much of it and things get a bit overblown. The safest route is to confine lace trims to the simplest of schemes and furnishings, so that the lace itself provides the decoration rather than accentuating other patterns. Plain white cotton pillowcases, neat waffle hand towels, traditional linen table napkins and crisp plain cotton curtains can all be lifted by a touch of white, cream or coffee-coloured lace. One of the prettiest ways to use it is as decoration for a lampshade. You can either trim an existing shade or make a new one from plain linen.

To make a lace-trimmed lampshade

1 Starting with a basic wire frame, cut a shade to fit it from self-adhesive lampshade parchment. (To create your template, roll the frame across the parchment so that the shape leaves an imprint.)
2 Peel away the adhesive covering and lay a piece of plain linen over it. Press it carefully in place to fix it, then trim it to fit the parchment, leaving an extra 1cm (⅜in) of linen at the top edge.
3 Bend the shade into shape, with the linen on the outside, and glue the side edges together with a glue gun. You can now slip the shade over the frame, folding over the linen flap at the top and gluing it inside.
4 Use your lace to trim the bottom edge of the shade, or both the top and bottom, attaching it neatly with the glue gun. Deeper scalloped pieces will work well along the bottom, and narrower pieces can be used for the top. You may find it's

Left: Traditional tea-stained lace makes a delicate edging for a plain linen lampshade.

best to cut the lace into sections so that you can get it to lie flat against the shade without stretching or pleating.

Q I have acquired a beautiful embroidered silk mandarin-style coat which I will never wear but would love to display. How can I do this without damaging the fabric?

A The colours and shapes of antique clothes make beautiful display items as well having their own interesting past. If you can get hold of a traditional tailor's dummy, this will be a good way to recreate the original look of the coat and preserve its shape. A simpler method, however – and a way of accentuating the design more graphically – is to thread it onto a pole and mount it on the wall. Hanging is not a good idea for items such as bias-cut dresses and heavily beaded designs, which may be pulled out of shape or torn by the weight, but it's ideal for stronger pieces, because it avoids the pressure damage from other clothes and the crease marks that might be caused if you kept the coat folded away.

You need to check it for moth and other damage first, and make sure that the shoulders and arms, which will bear the weight of the coat, are in good condition. Then cut a length of narrow wooden dowelling, and tape or bind upholstery wadding (batting) or foam around it to pad the wood. Thread the dowelling through both arms of the coat (the high neckline should hide the pole) so that the arms are outstretched, with the ends of the pole just visible at each wrist. You can now hook the pole ends onto large cuphooks screwed into the wall. Be careful to avoid a position in direct sunlight that might fade or weaken the fabric, and slip a couple of lavender sachets or other moth repellents into the arms to protect it from future damage.

Q What's the best way of storing clothes and furnishing fabrics to avoid moth damage and permanent creases?

A Your simplest defence against moths is to keep fabrics moving, rather than letting them stay in one place providing a nice cosy breeding ground for the larvae that do the damage. Even if the fabrics aren't in active use, take them out of storage now and then, give them a good shake and an airing, and smooth out any creases and folds before you put them away again (wrapping anything particularly precious in acid-free paper, see page 00). Keep them clean, too: moths are more likely to breed in dirty fabrics, so pieces that have been freshly laundered or dry-cleaned will be less at risk. (For the same reason curtains need to be kept clean, and their folds shaken out regularly to make sure they're not harbouring either the moth or its eggs.)

The other benefit of such treatment is that it will help prevent the formation of creases, which ultimately weaken fabric and leave permanent marks. It's to prevent creases that you should always roll fabrics rather than folding them.

Moths go for wool and thick, textured fabrics in which they can burrow – smooth, silky surfaces are less at risk. The traditional way to repel moths was to store clothing and textiles in cedarwood chests along with sachets of herbs such as orris root, woodruff, southernwood or lavender. Mothballs made of camphor or more modern chemical alternatives are very strong-smelling and it's difficult to get rid of the scent, but cedarwood and herbs like lavender smell sweeter and less 'medicinal', making their use more a pleasure than a remedy. Add little bags of lavender flowers among your clothes or look out for cedarwood balls or 'natural botanical' anti-moth sachets containing potent mixtures of lavender and other herbs.

Q I've bought two old matching bedspreads from a flea market, simply because the fabrics are so lovely. They really need to be kept as a pair, but I haven't a room with twin beds.

A With a matching pair, the obvious thing is to turn them into curtains. The length will give you enough fabric for a beautifully long drop, and if the bedspreads have any faded patches these will be less noticeable among the folds. The only questions are whether to line them and how to hang them.

The type of fabric will partly determine whether the curtains will need to be lined. With damask and other fabrics that have a subtle pattern worked into the weave, you'll find that this can be seen to best effect with the light behind it. Therefore any lining you add should be relatively lightweight in order not to block it completely. One option is to add temporary linings that complement or contrast with the colour of the main fabric. By attaching the linings with press studs (snaps) along the top, or with a row of buttons for a neat button-through finish, you will be able to detach and swap them to match the seasons, or perhaps to leave the curtains unlined in summer.

The simplest heading is to use café clips, which can be clipped directly onto the fabric and slotted onto a pole or rail (though these are recommended only for lightweight, unlined curtains). If the reverse side or lining is suitable, you could create a decorative effect with an integral valance, which is also a good way of using up excess fabric to fit a shorter window. Simply fold over the tops of the curtains and attach to the pole with café clips, or with ribbon ties stitched to the fold at regular intervals.

Left: Old bedspreads provide good-sized panels of fabric perfect to use for instant curtains.

Q Is there any way of removing ingrained marks, such as rust, wine or candle wax, from old fabrics?

A It depends partly on the material itself and partly on how valuable the item is. In general, cottons and linens are fairly robust, whereas fabrics such as silk and wool are much more delicate and won't stand up to harsh cleaning techniques. But don't take risks with pieces you care about: ask for an expert opinion rather than tackling it yourself.

Rust marks
Tiny reddish-brown marks are sometimes found in old garments where dressmaking pins, left in the fabric after sewing or altering, have rusted. A traditional cleaning method is to cover the mark with lemon juice and fine salt, leave for an hour, then rinse and launder the fabric. If the rust is deeply ingrained, though, it may be too late to shift the mark, in which case your only options are to cut the piece out or learn to live with it. If it's a special item, such as a christening gown or antique piece, take it to a professional for invisible mending. Otherwise it may be best to accept the damage as part of the garment's history.

Tea and wine stains
Cotton damask — the kind used for traditional table linen — is usually pretty tough, and some experts recommend that you take the plunge and wash it in boiling water to remove stains. If you don't feel brave enough, or if you suspect your damask is too old for such rough treatment, try sponging the marks with a solution of equal parts of water and glycerine.

Candle wax
Scrape off as much of the wax as you can using your fingernail or a palette knife or spatula, then dissolve the remaining wax by dabbing it with a linen cloth dipped in methylated spirit (denatured alcohol).

Q I'm planning to use a second-hand kilim as a bedroom rug. Is there any way of checking its provenance and quality?

A The flat-woven rugs known as kilims have been made in the Middle East and Central Asia for centuries, traditionally from hand-spun wool dyed with natural colourings extracted from plants and insects. The fabric was originally designed to be used for practical items such as bags and curtains. For nomadic cultures, what mattered most was that it was tough and wind-resistant, and at the same time lightweight and flexible enough to be rolled or folded while travelling. But the commercial possibilities were recognized during the second half of the 20th century, when the colours and patterns became popular among Western travellers and interior decorators. After this, factory-spun wools and chemical dyes started to take over in some areas,

although contemporary demand for earthy colours and traditional techniques has led to a return to older methods.

Because the symbolic motifs woven into the patterns have been handed down through the centuries, and because the nomadic lifestyle of the kilim-makers keeps them on the move, it's difficult to pin down the age or source of any particular rug. Genuine antiques will be extremely expensive, but contemporary kilims may still be well made and authentically coloured. The thing to check is the quality of the wool fibre: make sure this is soft and strong rather than short and frizzy. And remember that it wasn't designed only with the floor in mind: think back to its more versatile roots and experiment with other uses, such as curtains, wall hangings, bedcovers and tablecloths.

A valuable kilim that is in need of repair should be taken to a specialist for mending. A cheaper weave, however, can be tackled by anyone confident with a needle, either binding any fraying edges with yarn in blanket stitch, or using a 'stopper stitch' in string or heavy thread to prevent the edges from unravelling further. To work a stopper stitch, find the warp threads (between which the pattern is woven) and catch the string around these, two or three at a time, tying each cluster with a small knot before threading the needle along the fabric edge to the next one.

Individual marks on a kilim can be spot-cleaned with mild detergent, as you would treat a wool carpet. Be sure to test for the fastness of the dyes first, by dabbing with a damp white handkerchief to see if it picks up any colour. The dyes are more likely to bleed in cheaper rugs. To clean the whole rug, test the dyes for fastness, then submerge the kilim in a bath and wash it gently

Left: Second-hand kilims can be used as tablecloths, curtains, bedcovers and wallhangings as well as providing traditional floor coverings.

with mild soapsuds. Pick a warm, sunny day so that you can dry it in the open air – it must dry thoroughly to eliminate any risk of the fibres rotting. To ensure that it holds its shape while drying, nail the rug flat onto a wooden backing (an old door is perfect).

Q I've found a very pretty Victorian-style sampler, which is dated 1860 but is, I'm sure, nowhere near that age – especially as it was very inexpensive. Is it worth framing?

A Genuine samplers are highly sought-after, so you're unlikely to find any real bargains. Even basic school samplers, worked in plain colours during the 19th century so that pupils could practise letters and numerals along with their needlecraft, are relatively expensive, and earlier pieces with fine stitching and more elaborate decoration are museum quality. Among the most valuable is whitework; popular in the 17th and 18th centuries, it is stitched in white thread on white fabric, with panels cut away and filled with needle lace.

Part of the charm of an antique sampler is the history it holds: the maker's name and age (although this was sometimes discreetly unpicked later) as well as the date of the sampler itself. If it hasn't been well cared for, stains and moth holes may lower the value, but they don't detract from the historical interest. If it's genuine, it needs professional cleaning by a conservator and careful framing. Make sure it is mounted on linen or acid-free paper (see pages 148-156) and covered with glass, and don't hang it where sunlight or moisture can fade or stain the fabric.

Modern copies can still be attractive for display purposes. Although often worked from mass-produced kits, they are usually based on original designs, and because they involve hand-stitching, they have a sense of individuality. Also, the colours, though often muted, are generally not as faded as antique samplers, which can sometimes look almost monochromatic.

wood

There's a familiarity about wood that makes us feel naturally at home. Where glass and ceramics present us with fragile surfaces and an obvious vulnerability, wood feels solid and manageable. Not only is it robust enough to stand up to everyday use and amateur restoration work, but it is also versatile enough to use in any room. Despite its unchanging image, wood can provide extraordinary variety: it is as capable of creating sleek, formal elegance as warm, mellow simplicity. Domesticity comes in many forms, and wood will adapt to most of them, from floorboards and panelling to furniture and kitchen accessories, with surfaces that can be matt or polished, plain or decorated, neutral or painted.

You need an open mind when shopping for wooden items. There are few bargains left in traditional polished furniture, and even the simpler, farmhouse-style pieces are often overpriced. The trick is to sharpen your imagination to see beyond the obvious. If you can spot innovative ways in which to recycle flea market objects, you'll be able to beat the dealer to all sorts of unexpected treasures. Tackle basic renovation work yourself – wood is more forgiving than many materials – but if you suspect a piece has any value, ask for expert advice.

Q Can I create a floor out of old boards bought from a salvage yard? What problems might I face?

A Reclaimed flooring has obvious environmental benefits and is usually fairly economical to buy, although you may need professional help in laying the boards – especially if they are of different thicknesses. If at all possible, you should try to find boards that have come from a single floor, not only to ensure that the type of wood and colour is uniform but to avoid the problem of unevenness. It doesn't matter too much if the boards vary in width – in fact, this will add historical interest – but it's much more difficult to achieve a satisfactory finish with boards of different thicknesses. Even if you place packing on the supporting joists beneath thinner boards, or plane the underside of thicker ones, some will inevitably stand slightly proud of the floor.

The wood will vary according to the original source of the timber. Boards from town houses are likely to be pine; if they came from a church you might find yourself with pitch pine, which was often used for pews and pulpits; whereas country timber might be oak or elm – or whatever grew locally at the time. Whatever the wood, though, it's important to store the boards in situ for at least a week before attempting to lay them, so that they can become accustomed to the heat levels and atmosphere of the room.

To make the most of the natural character of the wood, don't sand your new floor: this would simply take off the entire top surface and leave you with white wood that you might as well have bought new. Instead, strip it to reveal the grain of the wood – you can do this yourself by scrubbing with household caustic soda (wearing rubber gloves). Then, rather than varnishing it, give it a couple of coats of finishing oil. This will penetrate the grain, leaving you with a lovely mellow surface that repels water stains but is still natural-looking. If you want to create more of a sheen, wait a few months and then wax it.

Right: Reclaimed wooden boards will make an elegant new floor, with a beautiful natural grain that can be enriched with beeswax.

CARING FOR WOOD FURNITURE

○ Most wood responds badly to a very dry environment, drying out and shrinking, which weakens the structure of the piece. Central heating is generally unfriendly, but you can help matters by not placing furniture near direct heat sources.

○ Don't polish too frequently, just when marks need to be buffed out. Use a good furniture wax (containing beeswax), applying it sparingly with a clean dust cloth and buffing the finish with another.

○ To move furniture, always lift it straight up. Don't tip the piece backwards as this can put too much strain on legs and other joints.

REMOVING MARKS FROM WOOD

Think twice before you remove every sign of wear: all second-hand pieces will have some mark of their history and this is part of their charm. Lacquered or varnished surfaces will need specialist treatment, but less highly polished surfaces will respond to a few home remedies.

○ Bruising: Marks caused by accidental knocks can be eased if you soak them with a wet sponge for 15 minutes so that the surface expands back into shape.

○ Burns and scorch marks: The only effective remedy is to sand off the surface, so you may prefer to live with the mark.

○ Red wine stains: These can't be removed completely, but you can lighten the mark by scrubbing gently with warm, soapy water.

Q How can I tell whether there is still active woodworm in an old pine cupboard? It has the telltale boreholes, but does that mean the infestation is now over? If so, is it safe to use the cupboard without fear of the worm spreading to other furniture?

A Woodworm is actually a beetle rather than a worm, and it is the grubs that cause the harm. The beetles lay their eggs in cracks and damaged surfaces, and the grubs then eat their way out through the wood, creating channels that weaken it and leaving small piles of sawdust as they go. You're most likely to find it in cheaper woods such as pine and beech, and particularly in badly cared-for furniture that provides cracks and gaps in which the beetles can breed. If the exit holes look clean and 'woody', or a lot of fresh-looking dust appears when you tap them, it suggests that the beetles are still active. In that case, the wood will need treating with a proprietary insecticide – you should be able to find a low-odour, transparent wood treatment. Saturate the entire piece by spraying all over, leaving for a few minutes, then spraying again so that you get twice the saturation. (Work outside if possible, or at least make sure your working area is well ventilated. Wear a filter mask and protect the floor with newspaper or plastic sheeting.)

If the holes don't look particularly new, you are probably safe for the moment. However, have a good look at the condition of the joints; if you

woodworm detective

If you are wondering whether a piece is genuinely old or has been cobbled together from other furniture parts, woodworm traces can provide a clue. It's only when the beetles actually emerge that they create those neat round holes; under the surface they will be churning up a maze of tunnels causing widespread damage. If you notice suspect channels on the surface of the furniture, it means that the wood has either been cut through and reused in different sections, or planed right back from its original surface.

can replace split pieces and close gaps by fixing any damaged joints, you will make it much harder for a new infestation to start. It's a good idea to treat joints, and raw wood such as the underneath of tables and the inside of drawers, with insecticide for extra protection. Woodworm can reappear – even in furniture that has been dipped in caustic soda – so it's worth taking precautionary action and making a quick annual check for new holes in late spring.

Q Old (and sometimes not so old) pine furniture is the most common type found in flea markets, but using a lot of wood of the same tone seems to have a deadening effect on interiors. How easy is it to disguise the surface with paint or other decoration?

A Prepare the surface of the wood by sanding it to give it a good 'key' to which the paint can adhere. So long as the wood has been previously finished with wax or varnish, there will be no need for you to prime it to prevent the paint from sinking right into the grain, but you will still need to apply a base of undercoat. (Apart from anything else, this saves you from wasting paint by discovering that you need more than one top coat to cover the grain of the wood.)

Now add your colour, using eggshell – or emulsion (latex) plus a coat of clear varnish – for a subtle, semi-matt finish. Be careful with gloss finishes: if you have more than a few pieces in one room, their high polish can start to look very glaring and institutional. The colours you use depend on the effect you want to create and the style of the furniture you are decorating.

❍ Simple, square-cut pieces respond well to muted, earthy colours – grey, taupe, ochre and russet – for a Shaker-style effect.

❍ Prettier, more decorative designs may be better suited to light-reflecting, pastel shades, recreating an elegant Gustavian look.

❍ For a more individual angle, create your own freehand designs, painting your furniture with panels of colour or with abstract and geometric shapes against a plain background. Or take inspiration from the Bloomsbury group and decorate it with offbeat, painterly motifs in soft yellows, pinks and blue-greys.

Below: Painting kitchen chairs in fresh colours is a quick way of updating plain second-hand pine.

Q I've picked up a couple of dark-stained doors with some very elaborate grain patterning. I can't decide whether to keep the grain design or strip them back – what do you suggest?

A Back in the 17th century, people used this technique regularly to make plain softwood look like expensive oak or walnut. After adding a darker stain, they used artist's tools to 'grain' the colour and create detailed artificial knots. The result was often stylized rather than realistic, with flamboyant waves and swirls worked into the surface. This effect continued to be popular through the next few centuries – including a revival of the technique in the 1920s and '30s – right up to the present. In recent times, mass-produced kits have been developed to supply colourwashes and graining tools to help you add a wood-effect finish to machine-cut MDF (medium-density fibreboard) and other flat surfaces.

The trouble with removing old graining is that, if the wood beneath is in poor condition, you may be in for a big disappointment and a lot of further restoration work in order to create a decent surface. On the other hand, if the wood is good or is of historical value, then the process of stripping it back may do lasting damage. So either way you could be causing more harm than good. What you need to do is to assess, first, the age and value of the doors themselves and, second, whether or not the artificial graining has any historical or artistic interest in its own right. If you suspect that the doors are old or valuable then

you'd be unwise to attempt any sort of restoration without consulting an expert. And you might well decide that the grained finish – even if considerably newer than the original doors – has its own place in their story and should be preserved for its own interest.

Q Lengths of decorative carved architrave (moulding) often crop up in salvage yards. They are very beautiful but look rather unwieldy; how can they be incorporated into the home?

A In these days when so many architectural details are available mass-produced from moulded wood, plaster or even glass-fibre, it's criminal not to make use of the real thing when you come across it. Old carved wood surrounds from doors and windows will often be too hefty or elaborate to reuse in their original form (or for their original purpose, for that matter) but if you think laterally you will find a host of other destinations in which to direct them.

How you use them depends partly on the weight of the wood. Some architrave will be fashioned from slim sections that were simply attached to the surface of supporting timbers to add interest. This can be used as decoration – applied to shelf and table edges almost like a veneer or fixed across dresser or plate-rack tops – and used to create window pelmets (cornices), its light weight easy to hold with panel pins or a good wood glue. Other architrave will be more substantial, however: it will need strong supports beneath it, but can be used for all sorts of interesting effects and furnishings. Use lengths of it as bookshelves; stand a length on bricks or on stone pedestals to create a decorative bench that will stand against a wall; or use a particularly fine section as a mantelpiece for an unusual fireplace.

---

print paraphernalia

Look out for printers' lettering blocks, and for the wooden cabinets or drawers that would once have held them. These wide, shallow drawers, divided into masses small compartments, make useful display cases if hung on the wall, and the individual letters, sometimes highly decorative, can be used to stamp a name or initial into books and other possessions.

Right: An original length of carved wood architrave makes a splendid mantelpiece for a country fireplace.

Q I have picked up a collection of items – a tailor's dummy and a set of wooden shoe lasts – that must have come from some sort of couturier's shop. How can I put them to decorative use?

A These are wonderfully elegant shapes, and although they were never designed for a decorative purpose, the best of them can be as beautiful as carved wooden sculptures. Both originally fulfilled the practical function of allowing clothes to be individually fitted, with polished wooden parts braced together by metal brackets that could be adjusted to increase or decrease the size of the pattern. You might also find wooden hat blocks from the same source – a good way to store hats without the damage that can be caused if you rest them on the brim.

Shoe lasts haven't much practical domestic use, but these heavy, intriguingly shaped tools can find new purpose as doorstops or just as decorative pieces. The traditional tailor's dummy, on the other hand, has evolved into the modern shop window mannequin and therefore becomes the perfect way to display special clothes. You are very unlikely to come across any of the original articulated designs, made from solid wood and with movable joints; but simpler versions, with either cotton or linen stretched over the frame and a wooden spindle running from top to toe through the middle, are more frequent finds. Use them in place of coat hooks and hat stands: the gentle curves will support the weight of a favourite coat and help to keep it in shape. Or follow the shop window example and use the dummy to display a well-cut dress (but be careful with fragile or heavily decorated fabrics – see page 23). Dress it with scarves and necklaces for a combination of storage and display, or just let it stand as a sculpture, dramatic and contoured against a plain wall.

Left: Traditional shoe lasts fixed to the wall make intriguing clothes hooks for a bedroom or bathroom.

Q I've bought a tiny chest of drawers – less than 30cm (1ft) across – which is a perfect replica of the real thing but too big for a doll's house. I'm intending it as a christening present for a godchild, but what would have been its original use?

A Craftsmen's miniatures (also known as apprentice's pieces) are delightful things and can be put to all sorts of uses. They were originally made as exhibition pieces, to demonstrate the craftsman's skill and, it's sometimes thought, as prototypes of full-size furniture designs. As well as chests, you can sometimes find more elaborate designs complete with jointed doors so that they look like miniature wardrobes. They can be surprisingly expensive for their size – especially if made of more valuable woods such as mahogany or walnut. This is because, despite the small amounts of wood involved, the work itself demanded just as much accuracy and even more intricacy, often demonstrating elaborate inlay or marquetry. If you can find cheaper pine pieces, however, these make excellent jewellery, sewing, spice and document boxes. Children find them a fun place to stash their treasures, and they look very pretty in children's rooms.

If the wood is not particularly special, or is in less than perfect condition, you can renovate miniature boxes and chests such as these with your own choice of decoration or colour. Paint and découpage designs can be used to match them to your furnishings or to create personalized decoration, and they can be labelled with the owner's name or with the items they are to hold.

keeping drawers running smoothly

The most likely cause of jammed drawers is overloading – which can be a problem in miniature chests as well as in full-size designs. If the drawers stick even when sensibly filled, try rubbing white candle wax onto the runners to help them slide more smoothly.

Q Interesting artefacts such as kitchen utensils always look very appealing in old wood, but how can they be prevented from splitting and discolouring?

A Wooden kitchenware can be made from anything from sycamore or beech to box or fruitwood. It is a type of 'treen' (literally 'made from trees'), a term that originally meant the skilfully crafted domestic items made from carved or turned wood from the 16th century onwards – everything from simple goblets and candle holders to more elaborate tobacco jars, powder boxes and wig stands in quality woods. Today, however, it has come to include more basic pieces such as breadboards and rolling pins, which are easier to come by.

Wooden kitchenware that you want to use for serving or preparing food obviously needs to be seasoned with non-toxic oil. Breadboards and salad bowls can be rubbed with olive oil – or walnut oil, which will feed the wood, bringing out its grain and colour, while remaining flavourless. Both of these will need to be renewed frequently, but for a longer-lasting treatment try using tung oil. This traditional Chinese recipe is thick and viscous, like treacle, and very resistant to water.

Q The unexpectedness of outdoor items used indoors always creates interesting contrasts. Can you suggest practical ways to recycle outdoor timbers such as ladders and gates for domestic use?

A Strong architectural shapes lend structure to home furnishings, especially in plain painted rooms, where their dramatic lines will have the most impact. Items like ladders and gates, which are essentially practical, can transfer very naturally to domestic use if you look for pieces of the right size and scale, and think imaginatively about where they will work best.

Traditional wooden ladders often end up on the second-hand market because their working life depends so much on sound condition: any weakness in the wood or the joints leaves them too dangerous for normal use. With a little attention to any loose rungs or damaged wood, however, they are perfect for lighter, more decorative purposes.

❍ One of their simplest uses is as bathroom towel rails. Contemporary towel rails are often fashioned to emulate the ladder design, but if you have the real thing, so much the better. Make sure the wood is well scrubbed or sanded so that the cloth won't catch on it, and lean it securely against the bathroom wall. Particularly elegant, if you can find them, are orchard ladders, which taper towards the top.

❍ Use a ladder as a self-contained picture gallery – this is the perfect way to display a collection of matching small prints or framed photos. Screw a pair of curtain hooks to the underside of each rung, and hang a picture from the rung by attaching a corresponding pair of hooks to the top of each picture.

❍ Wooden gates can serve as unusual display and hanging racks when fixed to the wall, especially if weathered and worn so that their timbers take on an attractive bleached, driftwood appearance. Hang the gate on strong hooks, or screw it firmly into studs in the wall, then fix additional hooks or nails to the struts so that the wooden framework creates an interesting background for coats, hats and scarves.

Right: An old wooden gate creates an unusual hat rack for both display and storage.

CLEANING PATTERNED WOOD SURFACES

Remember that surfaces such as marquetry and inlay aren't completely smooth. Don't use a duster on them, because individual pieces of the pattern may snag it, trapping fibres or bending back the veneer. The best thing to use is a soft brush.

TO REPAIR MARQUETRY

1 Make a template by laying a piece of paper over the gap and rubbing around the edges with a pencil (gently, as the wood will bruise easily).

2 Now lay the template on your new piece of wood (making sure the grain runs in the right direction) and carefully cut around the shape with a fretsaw (scroll saw), tapering the edges away slightly behind the surface so that the piece will fit more neatly into its space.

3 Using a small brush, apply a thin layer of specialist cabinet maker's glue to the back of the veneer and to the empty space. Press the new piece firmly into place, and immediately wipe away any excess glue.

---

wooden bedheads

Look out for old wooden bedheads, sometimes sold separately from their original frame. These can be painted, or covered with fabric or découpage patterns, and then added to an existing plain divan to give it more character.

Q I've found a little table with a wooden marquetry top. It's very pretty but part of the inlaid design is missing: can it be repaired without looking botched?

A The name marquetry comes from the French 'marqueter' (to inlay) and 'marque' (a mark). The effect can also be created with materials such as ivory or metal, but different-coloured woods produce the subtlest finish, with contrasting shades defining a gentle pattern over the surface. These designs, first seen in the 17th century, are detailed and delicate, so it's important that your repair is deftly worked – otherwise you might be better off leaving the pattern incomplete and letting its age speak for itself.

Marquetry patterns aren't inlaid into a background but are actually created from pieces of veneer – usually about 1.5–3mm ($\frac{1}{16}$–$\frac{1}{8}$in) thick – butted up to one another like a jigsaw to cover the entire surface. The first difficulty is to match exactly the colour of the pieces that are missing; the second, to fit the new pieces neatly so that the joins aren't obvious. Modern, much thinner veneers – more likely to be about 0.8mm ($\frac{1}{32}$in) thick – are available from timber suppliers, so if you hunt carefully you should be able to find a suitable grain and colour. The missing pieces can then be fitted by taking an impression of the gap (see panel on left).

Q How can I turn an old cable reel into a usable table?

A The things you're talking about are like giant cotton reels (thread spools), with two flat circular pieces joined by a central cylinder that makes a sort of pedestal if the reel is turned on its side. Usually made of scrapped softwood – remnants from the timber industry – and discarded by boatyards, engineering firms and so on, they are ideal for recycling into rough-finished tables, for use both indoors and out. It's simply a matter of rolling them into position.

Because of their industrial origins, they will

frequently be marked with company names or other lettering, and it's up to you whether you preserve this as part of the table design (by scrubbing it down and then sealing with a few layers of clear varnish) or transforming with a coat of paint. It depends on what sort of effect you want to create. Fresh watercolours such as blues and greens will combine with the nautical

Above: A giant, rough-finished industrial cable reel can be pressed into service as a rustic side table.

feel of the wood to conjure up a seaside theme. Smaller reels painted in bright primary colours are perfect for children's rooms, while plain wood will emphasize the table's recycled nature.

Q I've found a couple of carved and painted birds. How old are they likely to be and why were they made?

A Decoy birds were originally devised as hunters' lures in North America. The aim was to produce an impression, rather than a replica, of a particular bird, but they gradually became more realistic in design, with intricate carving, precise paintwork and sometimes glass eyes, from the mid-19th century onwards. During the 20th century, as hunting became a sport rather than a livelihood, many professional hunters swapped shooting for woodcraft and making decorative birds, so entire flocks of decoys have ended up in the collectors' market.

Decoy birds are most closely associated with colonial America, but they were first devised by the Native Americans. In addition, decoys of wader birds were made in France's Camargue region, and British wood-pigeon decoys were produced from the mid-19th century.

Decoys vary enormously in value, but it's tricky to identify their age and origin unless you've a practised eye. Some of the finest – including ducks, geese and swans – were made in the United States during the 1920s and 1930s, but modern craftsmen are producing attractive copies with the same simple lines and muted colours. Signs of genuine wear (such as shot marks), which will make the piece more interesting, also have the effect of reducing its cost. So, although it probably won't prove an investment as a collector's item, as long as you like the design and enjoy the sense of history attached to it, you shouldn't go wrong.

Q What's the best way of protecting painted woodwork? I've bought a set of very pretty painted chairs and I don't know how to restore the decoration.

A Painted woodwork of any age is charming, but how you tackle yours does depend on how old they are. If they look like contemporary pieces, and you are reasonably competent with a paintbrush, you could retouch any damaged decoration with plain emulsion (latex) or with artist's gouache, and then give the chairs a coat of clear varnish to protect the finish.

Older pieces, which may be valuable, need more care. If the seats are cane, that suggests a longer history. Tap the surface of the wood, too: it's possible that the chairs are not solid wood, but papier mâché moulded onto a wood or metal frame; in that case they could be 19th century, as this technique was popular with the Victorians. If you suspect this, and the decorative paintwork looks fragile, don't attempt any cleaning or restoration work without consulting an expert.

Q I love the traditional shape of garden trugs (baskets) but as I haven't a garden I can't really justify buying them. How else could I use them?

A The shallow, scooped-out design of these old-fashioned garden baskets originated 1,000 years ago in Sussex, England. The classic trug, still hand-crafted today using the original woods and techniques, is fashioned from curved slats of willow (the wood used for cricket bats). The rims and handles are made from sweet chestnut, usually with its bark left on to create the traditional rustic effect. Some of the newer versions are made from birch aircraft ply and, apart from the fact that these tend to be available in larger sizes, it's not always easy to spot the difference. But the charm of the trug is its simple durability. In France, where trugs are usually shaped with a flat base rather than a curved one, you can sometimes see repaired ones with sections of old bicycle wheel acting as handles, emphasizing their down-to-earth practicality.

The shallow design of trugs is versatile as well as graceful – perfect for all kinds of storage. Use them in the kitchen to hold vegetables, utensils or spare tea towels. They will stand handily on a worktop, or can be hung from a ceiling beam if their contents aren't needed so frequently. Make the most of them in the natural setting of the garden shed to tidy away gloves, seed markers and reels of twine. Or line them with fabric and use them as knitting baskets, or to hold toilet paper rolls and spare linens in a bathroom.

Repairing trugs

Trugs should last for at least 40 years, but most owners will carry on using them rather than part with them when they start to show their age, so the chances are that by the time a trug finds itself on the second-hand market it will need a few repairs. The most common problem is that the slats of the basket work loose and start to spring apart. For a do-it-yourself repair, you can try steaming the trug over a kettle, or soaking it in water, then bending the wood back into position. Leave the trug to dry out naturally – never over a radiator. For a professional repair, contact one of the remaining trug manufacturers.

Left: Carved decoy birds and miniature craftsmen's chests are among the wooden pieces to look out for. When buying decoys, try to check for signs of genuine wear, such as shot marks, that authenticate their history.

paintings, prints and paper

The paper artefacts you can find in flea markets by the boxload are a mine of decorative possibilities, full of potential for adding colour and pattern, and with an adaptability that can shift their style from simple to sophisticated, depending on how you use them. If you feel wary buying paintings without any idea of their provenance, then start with inexpensive pictures, going for what you like and not worrying about perfect frames. Or concentrate on more homely materials such as postcards and posters. Try to develop an eye for what's worth buying by choosing an area of interest and making it yours –Victorian greetings cards, perhaps, or old maps – so you can learn to spot things instinctively among the clutter of the stall or shop and feel confident about how much you're paying.

If you buy a painting you want to know more about, take it to an impartial expert such as a local gallery or museum, who may be able to provide a history and conservation advice. But don't think of a flea market painting as a financial investment. Buy it because you love it.

Q I love traditional Victorian-style cards and scraps, and have amassed quite a collection. How can I use or display them?

A The Victorians took communication seriously and perfected it as an art form, forever sending each other cards or leaving them at each other's house after visits. Today we associate this endless exchange of courtesies and memoranda more with the world of work than with social life, but in those days ladies of leisure made it their business to keep in touch. Email may have revived the practice of writing rather than phoning, but that owes more to its speed and efficiency than to any pleasure in preparing and crafting the words. To the Victorians, the presentation mattered as much as the message.

Old greetings cards and postcards are common flea market finds and have become very collectable, particularly if they bear postmarks from interesting places or commemorating special events. There's always a certain fascination with their senders and recipients, and many collectors simply enjoy keeping their finds in albums or keepsake boxes, or perhaps framing them to create a wall display. But if some cards aren't in such good condition, or if you're not so sentimental about preserving memories intact, there are plenty of ways you can reuse them.

Turn them into new greetings cards by pasting the images onto stiff card or watercolour paper. Use pastel-coloured paper or layered sheets of flower-pressed giftwrap as your background for a traditionally romantic effect, or neutral-coloured recycled paper for a more rustic feel. Or you could use sections of thin plywood as your backing, to create an instant picture so that it's a present as well as a card. Trim your designs with ribbons, fabric scraps, dried flowers and leaves and send them for birthdays, St Valentine's Day, invitations and thank-you notes. Take advantage of all the distinctive computer typefaces available now to design your own message in suitable lettering – or learn traditional copperplate handwriting and impress all your friends.

If you don't like the thought of defacing the original handwriting, stamps and postmarks, look out for books of out-of-copyright ephemera – reproductions of traditional hearts-and-flowers illustrations and messages specifically designed to be cut out or photocopied.

Right: Use a collection of old postcards to make a decorative garland, letting the hand-written side create part of the design among the pictures.

Q I've recently bought a whole box of old postcards – the pictures themselves are nothing particularly special but they make intriguing reading. Is there a way of keeping them on show?

A The wonderful thing about old letters and postcards is that everyone used to know how to write – not flights of poetry, or even correct grammar necessarily, but elegant, flowing handwriting. Sometimes the script was genuine copperplate, but it was always shapely and legible. So if nothing else, you may want to frame the written side of your postcards – along with any attractively scripted letters and envelopes. But they are also perfect materials for decorating home office or writing desk accessories, especially if franked with interesting stamps and clear postmarks that authenticate their age and origin.

❍ If you want to use the cards themselves, and don't mind trimming some of them to fit, then use them to cover a plain wooden box to create a writing case or stationery holder. Lay a selection of cards, script side up, over the lid of the box and trim the edges where they overlap. Do the same around the sides of the box and paste them in place with PVA glue (white glue). To increase the antique effect, rub a little gilt cream around the exposed edge of the lid and top of the box.

❍ If you don't want to deface the actual cards, you can capture the style and nostalgia of their contents by photocopying them onto sheets of plain paper. This gives you the chance to pick out the most interesting bits – but also lets you hide any blots or smudges by slipping the corner of one card under another. Try to keep the effect random, though, by laying them at different angles and by contrasting different styles of writing before photocopying them onto large sheets. Use these to cover a plain wooden box or small chest of drawers, pasting it in place with PVA glue (white glue), then add a coat of matt varnish to seal the finish.

Q I've occasionally come across old wallpaper books for sale – they are full of tempting patterns, but as they're no longer in production I'm not sure what use they'd be. Any ideas?

A Those sample-size sheets of wallpaper, all neatly bound and kept flat and uncreased, are infinitely more useful than the scruffy offcuts from half-used rolls that end up in the attic or garage. Children have always used them for decorating doll's houses, but adults can make use of them too, with all sorts of decorating projects that are perfectly suited to the small amounts of paper on offer. Use sheets of pattern to wrap storage boxes and files to brighten up a study, or to cover picture and photo frames. Cut wallpaper panels to line dressing-table drawers or the backs of shelves, and frame small sections of pattern to hang on the wall as instant pictures. Or snip small squares of pattern and glue them onto stiff paper (watercolour paper is perfect) to make your own personally designed notecards.

But you can make the paper go quite a bit further if you use individual motifs to create a découpage pattern. This is a great way to use up bin-end rolls (or those half-rolls still lurking in the attic), because once the motifs are cut out and you're no longer limited to the scale of the printed pattern, you can position them as you want, to add decoration to furniture, walls and even floors.

1 Prepare your base surface and paint it with a couple of coats of emulsion (latex), or specialist floor paint if you're decorating a floor. If you use a colour that more or less matches the background of the wallpaper, you'll be able to create a very similar effect to the paper itself – and it also means you won't have to cut around the motifs so exactly.
2 Now snip around the motifs you want to use and work out your pattern – either following the arrangement on the original paper or creating a new one for yourself. If you are going to decorate a floor, seal the cutouts by coating both sides with

a 50/50 solution of PVA (white glue) and water to toughen them up; leave them to dry and then give them another coat.

3 Glue the motifs carefully in position with lightly diluted PVA (white glue), applied in a light, even coat, and leave to dry. (If you're working on a floor, apply another coat of the

Above: Wallpaper samples or offcuts can be used to line cupboards and shelves with pretty designs.

50/50 PVA mix over the entire area and leave to dry, then coat with several coats of clear water-based varnish.)

framing ideas

There's no limit to the items that will make an interesting display if you frame them, either singly or in groups. Don't feel restricted to paintings and photographs. Here are some ideas:

Postcards: Group them together in different styles – romantic, saucy, or those 1950s and '60s pictures immortalizing early days of foreign travel.

Greetings cards: Christmas, Valentine, birthday, anniversary and Mothering Sunday cards can all be framed to preserve special messages.

Stamps: You can leave stamps on their envelopes to incorporate the postmark and hand-written address, or make a collage of the stamps – either steam them off completely, or paint a water line around the stamp and postmark so that you can pull it away, leaving a gently torn edge.

Cigarette cards: Pre-1918 cards are sought-after, but there are cheaper images from a later period when they were produced in greater quantity.

Old theatre programmes: These are a great way to conjure up a bit of stage glamour as well as to preserve genuine memories of special occasions.

Q I bought an old oil painting at an auction recently. It's nothing special, but I'd like to keep it in good condition – should I worry that it isn't glazed?

A Auctions, especially country sales, are good places to pick up art bargains. Inexpensive paintings are sold off in job lots, and as taste is so personal, you could find yourself more or less a lone bidder. It's sometimes worth it for the frames alone, and you'll often find one picture that you really like among three or four batched together.

Don't worry about the lack of glass – that, too, is a matter of taste. Although glazing would provide some protection against heat, damp and over-strong light, it's not really needed if the picture is varnished – and it has some practical disadvantages. Many people prefer to leave oils unglazed because glass creates glare and reflection that distract the eye and get in the way of the picture itself. Rather than relying on a glazed front to do the job for you, pay more attention to the hanging environment, as follows:

Light shouldn't be too strong. A certain amount of natural sunlight is good for oil paintings, as it enriches the colours (paintings left in dark cellars and attics get distinctly drab), but you need to avoid harsh direct light. Don't hang the picture right opposite a window as it can darken the varnish and dry out the painting.

Damp will cause mould. Avoid rooms that suffer from condensation, such as kitchens and bathrooms. Don't hang your painting on a damp wall, and keep the air circulating. Paintings left shut up for months may develop mildew because the air becomes damp and stagnant.

Heat is just as much of a problem. Central heating is particularly bad as it dries out the air, so avoid hanging pictures over radiators and pipes. Also be careful with picture lights – don't fit them immediately above the painting as they can emit surprisingly fierce heat. (Worst of all are yo-yo changes in temperature because the painting will keep expanding and contracting, causing cracks and flaking in both picture and frame.)

Dirt will eventually damage the painting and the frame, especially if it is very acid. If there's an open fire or cigarette smoke, clean the picture regularly.

avoiding broken glass

If you do decide to glaze a painting, always tape across the glass while you're transporting it. That way, if the glass breaks, it will stay in place and won't tear the canvas with sharp edges.

Left: Old postcards and greetings cards can be framed to pretty effect, with panels of decorative paper used as borders.

Q I have a weakness for interesting old picture frames, but sometimes they're very neglected and battered. Should I try to renovate them?

A Be careful. It's easy to be seduced into buying fairly mediocre paintings if they're attractively framed – and it's often the battered, distressed state they're in that creates the charm. It's remarkable what the patina of age can do for very unremarkable art, so that an amateur still life painted on a piece of hardboard one Sunday afternoon 20 years ago acquires unexpected style and character. And there's always a chance that the frame itself is of value. Either way, it's rarely worth tampering with it. If it's valuable, you should leave it to the experts, and if it's not, then smartening it up could destroy its only real point of interest. So proceed with caution, assessing the basic structural condition of the frame first and then tackling cleaning and surface restoration as gently as possible.

Structure
The frame has a practical purpose as well as a decorative one: if the painting is on canvas it's the frame that holds the stretchers keeping it in shape. So it's worth checking that the joints haven't been weakened by past knocks, poor storage, an over-dry environment or the pull of the frame's own weight. If the joints are damaged, the whole thing can fall apart.

Damaged moulding
It's not a good idea to attempt to mend this yourself. If you want to have it professionally restored, keep hold of any broken pieces. As a temporary measure, you can fix them carefully in place using an easily reversible adhesive. But unless the moulding is particularly valuable, it's probably better left with a few characterful gaps here and there.

Gilding
Gilding is very sensitive to atmospheric conditions, because if the wood beneath expands or contracts, the gilding can crack and flake. It can be either oil- or water-based. To find out which yours is, rub gently with a damp cotton swab: if the gilding comes off, it's water-based and shouldn't be washed. The safest course is to dust it with a soft brush. Don't try to brighten up the entire frame, but if it's badly dulled, you could try retouching it in places with gilt cream rubbed on with a cloth to bring out the highlights.

Remember that picture and frame work

Q I've found an old picture with a chunky wooden frame that's the perfect size to use as a serving tray. How could I make it 'tea-worthy'?

A Picture frames can make excellent trays. If you're lucky enough to come across the right combination of attractive picture, sound glass and solid frame you may not need to do much to it at all. If the image itself is damaged or you would rather display it somewhere safer, you can simple remove it and replace it with an alternative, or with a panel of paper or fabric, beneath the glass.

The most important thing is that the frame and backing are robust enough to keep the whole structure secure. You may find that the backing is loose or missing: in that case, have a piece of MDF cut to the same size as a replacement. Once you are happy with the glass and surface image, fix the new back securely in place with nails or panel pins.

Above: An old picture frame makes the perfect surround for a traditional-style tray. Add a new MDF back if necessary to make the base.

inseparably together: it's the whole package that creates the pleasing effect. And if you fall in love with something you spot tucked away on a flea market stall, it probably means you like it the way it is — so don't spoil things by trying to change it too much.

printed music

Flea markets are usually a plentiful source of old printed music that can be cut into individual sheets and used for all kinds of decorative purposes. Use these pages of graphic black and white design to cover files, books and stationery boxes, or to paper one wall of a small room, such as a study or loo.

Q I've bought an oil painting that has obviously been hung or stored somewhere rather grubby in the past. Can I do anything to clean it up?

A Traditional home methods of cleaning oil paintings include rubbing with the cut surface of a potato, or with white breadcrumbs, or with a soft cloth dipped in warm milk. Most professional picture restorers will shudder at the thought of these 'amateur' remedies, so before you try any of them it's worth checking to make absolutely sure that your painting isn't of any real value. If you're going to end up taking it to an expert, you don't really want to have to explain that it's already been subjected to half the contents of your pantry.

As long as you're happy that you're not meddling with an Old Master, you can try a little gentle cleaning to remove the worst of the surface dirt without breaking through the varnish. Stop immediately if you realize that the varnish is flaking off or that you are removing any of the paintwork. Follow the instructions below and always test a small, unobtrusive area of the painting first.

TO CLEAN AN OIL PAINTING

1 First remove superficial dust by brushing the surface lightly with a soft brush, but take care that paint isn't flaking off too. Some experts also suggest that a vacuum cleaner nozzle on low power can help here. Don't let the nozzle actually touch the picture, but hold it so that it collects the dust that's swept away by the brush. If there are spots of mould caused by storage in a damp atmosphere, wait until the picture is thoroughly dried out (but let it dry naturally – don't try to speed it up with a heater or hair dryer) then take it outside and brush off the mould with a soft brush.

2 Now try cleaning an unobtrusive part of the picture as a test area. Choose a part of the image that is dense and busy, so that it won't show if you remove a little of the paint as well. Dab gently in a circular motion with cotton wool (absorbent cotton) or a soft facial tissue dampened with saliva. You could also use pure soapflakes dissolved in water – again applied with cotton wool (absorbent cotton) – or try the cut potato suggested by the old-fashioned housekeeping guides. If any of these methods removes paint as well as dirt, stop at once. If it seems to be cleaning off surface dirt quite effectively, carry on – but with caution.

3 If you don't seem to be making much impact, you could shift things up a gear by trying turps on a small area – but go even more carefully as this will be much tougher on the grime. Bear in mind that this approach may totally change the colour of the varnish and leave the painting much brighter. You may find that you preferred the patina of the old varnish after all.

Cleaning the glass

If the painting has glass that needs cleaning too, spray the glass cleaner onto the cloth, not onto the glass. Be careful not to let any residue collect in the corners of the frame – it's a good idea to hold a strip of card against the inner edge to prevent this. Some restorers recommend avoiding cleaning fluid and instead polishing the glass with scrunched-up newspaper, which should clean away surface dirt without leaving streaks. If the glass is very sticky (from being hung in a room where people smoke regularly, for instance) you could use a little methylated spirit (denatured alcohol) on a cloth, but be careful not to let it touch the frame or the painting, as it is very corrosive and will damage their surfaces.

unframed pictures

Paintings on board, which doesn't need to be stretched like canvas does, can look just as good without a frame at all. If you want to hang them on a wall, you could try adhesive discs stuck onto the back (like the type used to display a ceramic plate). But leaving them unframed allows you to use them in other ways, too. Small pictures will look equally effective propped on a shelf or mantelpiece, while a larger one can give the impression of being painted directly onto the wall if you slot it into an alcove, or use it as the backing for a set of shelves or a glass-fronted cupboard.

Below: The beautiful colours of oil on board don't need framing in order to make an impact. If there is no way to fix it to the wall, stand the picture on a shelf or console table instead.

Q Is there any way of safely mending a torn watercolour?

A Not on a do-it-yourself basis. This is why watercolours, unlike oil paintings, do need to be glazed (and their frames well sealed at the back). The glass provides invaluable protection against tears and scratches, as well as damp, insects and the brown spots known as 'foxing'. If you're lucky, the tear won't be too visible, especially once the picture is framed, whereas if you try to patch it up with tape or glue, you will simply draw attention to it and do lasting damage that not even a professional restorer will be able to repair. If the picture is valuable or the tear is very noticeable, you will need to consult an expert, who will either back it with conservation-grade paper, or repair localized patches with fine Japanese paper and starch paste. If you want to create a temporary mend in the meantime, use neutral-pH tape (from a supplier of framing or conservation materials), applying it very carefully on the back of the tear. This tape can be peeled off and won't leave marks, but will prevent further damage.

Left: Flea markets are a good source of old prints, watercolours and frames, but you need to treat them with respect and clean frames carefully.

Q Flea markets often sell old books of prints – sometimes in good condition, sometimes fairly battered. If the book is already damaged, could I cut out individual pages for framing?

A Most prints now sold individually in markets and second-hand shops started life in book form. Botanical and zoological prints, old maps and architectural drawings all make very effective pictures – but they once made very beautiful books, too. Don't continue the plunder. If the book is still relatively intact, resist the temptation to damage it any further. (Check with an expert to see if it can be re-bound: if the spine is broken or pages are falling out, tie the whole thing together with linen tape and take it to a restorer.)

One solution (if it can be done without forcing the spine) is to photocopy individual pages for framing. These prints (along with pages from books that have genuinely disintegrated beyond hope of repair) make great presents. They can also create an inexpensive but dramatic display if you group them in sets or choose a framing style that unites the collection. You could even paste them directly onto a painted wall to create a print-room effect in classic 18th-century style. Try plain black-and-white woodcuts against a warm yellow or red wall, linked by decorative paper motifs to give a trompe l'oeil effect of silk cord and tassels. (Cut-paper ornaments providing bows, rosettes, borders and friezes are available from specialist decorators.)

LOOKING AFTER WATERCOLOURS

○ Touch the paper as little as possible – the acidity in your skin will weaken it, and marks will be very difficult to remove.

○ To prevent further damage, frame watercolours with museum-quality, acid-free mounts. These prevent direct contact between the paper and the glass and maintain a layer of ventilation to stop condensation from forming.

○ Don't hang watercolours in strong sunlight.

○ Avoid cold exterior walls where possible as these may promote condensation and mould growth behind the glass.

○ Don't hang them near spotlights or radiators that will create warm air currents and cause the paper to dry out.

Q I recently came across an old photograph showing my street a hundred years ago. Is it possible to have copies made without the negative? And how can I prevent it from fading?

A Old sepia-toned photographs are a wonderful evocation of local and family history, and if you've got any favourite images it's a natural instinct to want to have copies made for others who know the people or places involved. The good news is that you'll also be helping to preserve your original copy, so go ahead: have several prints made so that you can give some away, frame another to keep on display, and store the first one safely away. Most good photo labs will be able to make copies for you, preserving the original sepia tones and digitally retouching any marks or scratches. Don't go to a high-street processor as most of them are only equipped to handle modern film materials. Choose a specialist and ask to see examples of their work before entrusting a special picture to them.

Q I love collecting old books, whatever their condition. Is it possible to replace damaged endpapers? And what's the best way of taking care of them?

A The beautiful marbled paper traditionally used for the linings of book covers has

LOOKING AFTER OLD PHOTOGRAPHS

○ Make sure your hands are clean, and be careful not to touch the emulsion side that bears the image (on negatives, this is usually the more matt side).

○ Don't try to laminate or mount the originals, and don't expose them to light for too long, as the image will fade. Have a copy made for display and keep the original safe.

○ Important pictures are best stored individually in archive-quality sleeves made from plastic or paper (but it needs to be unbuffered pH-neutral paper, not the shiny white semi-transparent paper often supplied for photos).

○ Albums should be interleaved with photographic conservation paper. Avoid the type with adhesive-coated pages and plastic oversheets that are in direct contact with the images.

○ Be careful when labelling the back of photos – write in HB pencil to leave minimal impressions and to avoid show-through.

always been surrounded by mystique. The marbling process, which involves raking and combing a layer of floating paint into swirled patterns, then laying a sheet of paper on top to pick up the design, originated in 12th-century Japan. It was developed by the Ottomans, and spread to Europe in the 16th century, where it was used for lining cupboards as well as binding books. By the 19th century, books with marbled end-papers were popular but craftsmen kept the technique secret to protect their trade – and it was then superseded by mechanical book production.

The craft has been revived over the last 30 years or so, however. If you want to marble your own paper there are books and courses to teach you how. But you might feel more inspired by going to a fine paper shop that sells ready-marbled sheets – along with specialist book-binding tools such as glues and sewing threads. Don't expect to be able to tackle bookbinding on a do-it-yourself basis – it's a highly skilled profession. But a shop like this will give you an idea of the kinds of paper available, so that you can see what a book conservator or specialist restorer could achieve. And the papers are bound to suggest a host of other uses, such as covering for boxes, or borders for items you want to frame.

Below left: Old photographs make effective groupings because of their similar colour tone. Frame several together so that they look like an authentic family collection.

LOOKING AFTER OLD BOOKS

○ When taking a book from a shelf, don't pull it by the top of the spine. Books should stand slightly towards the front of the shelf so that you can push back the two on either side and remove the one you want with thumb and forefinger.

○ Be careful not to force the book open wider than it wants to go, for example when photocopying it. Turn the pages carefully to avoid tearing delicate paper, and handle with clean hands so that you don't leave thumb prints.

○ If any pages are loose, make sure they're smoothed into place, with no protruding edges or corners that might get crushed or folded.

○ Dust your books regularly and protect them from direct light.

○ Write your name in pencil rather than pen. If the book has a paper dust jacket, look after this as it will increase the value (don't snip out the price).

leather

Leather has a natural smartness that is all the more attractive for its familiar, everyday quality. From the rich, polished conker-brown of traditional suitcases to the worn upholstery of an old leather chair, we're accustomed to thinking of it as something robust and practical that can be used, mended, cleaned and reused. Flea markets are rich hunting grounds for leather objects. There's a special sense of satisfaction in using an old trunk or briefcase marked with the original owner's initials, and wondering who they were.

There's a fine line, though, between enjoying its unpretentious good looks and exposing it to rough handling and harsh modern pollutants. Leather doesn't last for ever. Eventually, suitcase hinges will wear out, upholstery will tear and stitching will fray, so do what you can to extend their life expectancy by treating them with respect. Bear in mind that marks from water and other substances leave permanent stains, and use leather dressings and polishes with discretion. Before trying any renovating technique, always test a small area to see what effect it will have, and if the piece is old or valuable, consult a professional restorer.

Q I've found a comfortable, battered old leather armchair that must have come from someone's study, as it is marked with dark ink stains. Can they be cleaned off, or should I let them stay?

A It sounds as though you've answered your own question. The beauty of old leather is the patina that tells you its past, so it's a shame to obliterate that history just for the sake of smartening it up. But if you feel it's been seriously neglected, you can do quite a lot to bring it back to life without making it look too new.

Dust the chair with a soft brush, then patch-test a discreet area with a little white spirit (mineral spirits) on a cloth. If it starts to take off the colour, don't go any further, but if all that's coming off is dirt, it should be safe to carry on. This technique should remove grease marks and might help a little with your ink stains, although they're probably well ingrained by now. Go gently, and be prepared to vary your pressure according to the condition of the surface. Where it is sound, you can apply more force, but be careful in areas where the leather is worn or damaged (see notes on red rot in Cleaning and Caring for Leather, overleaf). Always work outside or in a well-ventilated room.

There are plenty of proprietary leather cleaners, but these are really designed for modern leathers. However, it's always worth checking second-hand furniture for any indication of the manufacturer. The worn-leather look is very much in vogue these days, so you may find that an apparently old chair is newer than you thought. If that's the case, contact the manufacturers to see if they make a suitable cleaning product.

Left: Enjoy the authentic patina of old leather and don't try to smarten it up too much.

---

saddle soap

Conservation experts advise against using saddle soap on household leather: it's designed for cleaning and toughening up working leather that is used every day and exposed to a lot of dirt. If you apply it to a soft leather chair it will eventually harden the leather and can cause it to deteriorate.

CLEANING AND CARING FOR LEATHER

Leather is more vulnerable than it looks. It will harden and crack in dry conditions; it can be scuffed, worn or torn if roughly handled; and it can succumb to rot. Try not to let it dry out, and avoid getting it very wet as water marks will stain.

Always test for adverse reaction before using any polish or leather 'feed'. If you're in any doubt about the possible effect, or you are dealing with something of value, consult a professional restorer rather than attempting it yourself.

Never use shoe polishes, which will leave pigment stains. And don't feel you have to keep 'feeding' it with leather dressing. Cleaning leather is very satisfying but it's probably doing you more good than it is the leather. Most dressings are oil-based and there's a limit to how much oil the leather can absorb, so you shouldn't apply them more often than every 18 months or so. As long as the leather is flexible, you can probably leave it alone.

Red rot When you're buying old leather, avoid items whose surface is flaking off as a reddish dust. This is known as red rot and it means the leather is self-destructing. It can be caused by a combination of the dyes used in the tanning process, or by the acidity resulting from frequent handling. It can also be caused by everyday air pollution – leather absorbs sulphur dioxide and this weakens the fibres so that they lose their structure and the surface layers start to disintegrate. Unfortunately, once red rot has set in, there's not much you can do to repair the surface. A specialist might be able to restore it slightly with a process that in effect re-tans the leather. If there's only a small area of rot and you want to deal with it yourself, you could try a mixture of 60 per cent castor oil and 40 per cent white spirit (mineral spirits), applied with a cloth. Let it soak in for 24 hours then add a little more castor oil.

Q I've collected several old suitcases and leather trunks. They're really too heavy to use for travelling, but I love the look of them. How else can I use them?

A The great thing about traditional cases is that their smart leather has the same polished glow and grained colour of wood furniture, so they're terribly easy to incorporate in a furnishing scheme. Think of them first as beautiful objects, and then as brilliant extra storage, and you'll soon find places to use them. Stack them in ascending order, stagecoach style, against a bedroom wall or on top of a wardrobe. Use larger cases and trunks as blanket boxes and side tables – and if they're packed full enough to provide good support for the lid, add a few cushions on top to turn them into window seats. Look out, too, for voluminous wardrobe trunks, which can be stood on end so that the lid opens like a cupboard – perfect storage for spare towels and bedlinen.

Q What's the best way to keep old suitcases in good condition? Is it possible to replace the leather corner shields if they have become very worn or scuffed?

A Suitcases are different from upholstery because their leather is meant to be firm, so don't become obsessed with trying to soften it up. The only bits that will be softer are the straps and other working parts, which need to be more flexible. The best thing to use on suitcases is a good-quality furniture wax, such as beeswax, which will help improve the water-resistance of the surface. It won't make it waterproof, though, so avoid getting the leather very wet – water marks will stain. Apply the wax with a cloth, but use only small quantities and be especially careful if the leather is damaged or has a heavily grained finish, such as goatskin. If the surface is textured, then wax that is applied too thickly can get into the fibres and turn them white, the end result being a speckled surface. Use the wax sparingly, and be prepared for the softer leather of the straps

Above: Leather chests and cases, with their attractive polished surfaces, provide alternative storage in bathrooms and bedrooms.

to end up looking slightly darker, as it will absorb more of the wax.

The fitted corner shields you find on traditional suitcases are difficult to replace because they are usually riveted and stitched into position from the inside, with the suitcase lining added afterwards, covering the fixings so that you can't get at them. What you may be able to do instead is tidy up scuff marks with acrylic wax (available from a conservation materials supplier).

traditional remedy for preserving old leather suitcases

Add 1 teaspoon of vinegar to about 3 litres (13 cups) of warm water and gently wash the leather with this using a new sponge. Dry it with a clean, soft chamois leather. Now whisk 2 egg whites with 2 teaspoons of genuine gum turpentine (available from hardware stores) and rub this into the dried leather using a soft, absorbent rag. Dry off the excess with a clean glass cloth. Add shine with beeswax when the leather is completely dry.

Q Is it possible to repair an old chesterfield sofa? It's missing several buttons and there's a split in the leather seat.

A The luxurious deep upholstery and decorative buttoning of the traditional chesterfield echoed the interior design of Victorian carriages. It's rare to find a genuine chesterfield still with its original leather upholstery (and even rarer for it to be in good condition). If it's authentic, it's definitely a job for the professionals. But even if it's a modern copy, which is much more likely, it's not an easy item to work on.

The first problem is that it's very difficult to replace missing buttons because you can't get access to them. To do it properly, you need to remove the leather from the back of the sofa and then use special needles to secure the new buttons in place, so this needs to be left to the professionals. The only way to short-cut the process is to glue the replacement buttons in position, which could provide a temporary solution. But there's an honest quality about old leather that demands honesty in its turn. It's an organic material with a natural-coloured finish, and doesn't react well to attempts to 'fake' it. It might be an interesting idea deliberately to use mismatched buttons – perhaps bright fabric-covered designs instead of subdued leather – to prove you're not attempting to fool anyone. But it would be an even better idea to leave the buttons missing as a sign of the sofa's age and authenticity.

Mending splits is tricky too, as it's only possible if you can get at the leather from the reverse, i.e. if it's nailed to the outside of the frame rather than held inside it. If you can, remove these nails then peel the leather gently back. Cut a piece of muslin slightly larger than the torn area, and brush it lightly with a weak solution of PVA glue (white glue). Press this carefully into place on the back of the leather so that the split edges are pulled together and perfectly aligned. After two hours, brush on another layer of glue, then, when it's dry, roll the leather gently back into place and re-nail it into the frame.

Q What is the best way of repairing worn stitching and damaged handles on old briefcases?

A The traditional style of leather document cases has barely changed for a hundred years or more, so old cases are never out of fashion – the more unusual ones simply have a sort of designer distinction that singles them out from the anonymous products of a modern luggage department. But they do wear out, and many of the second-hand cases available at flea markets are there because they've not much useful life left. Avoid them if the surface of the case is starting to disintegrate into red dust: this is red rot and you won't be able to repair it (see page 64). Handles are also at risk from rot because of constant contact with the skin, which is very acidic, but they can be replaced by leather restorers, good luggage departments and some saddlers. It won't be cheap, though, so it's not worth buying a case in generally poor condition and then relying on restoration work to make it usable.

If the stitching looks damaged, check that it's the stitches themselves that are coming loose, rather than the leather crumbling away between them. Again, if the leather is rotting, you won't be able to do anything about it. Stitching, however, can be repaired. For a long-term solution you should go to a professional, who will use special stitching techniques, but you could try a temporary do-it-yourself mending job using waxed cotton thread and strong needles. Proceed carefully and try to follow the patterns of the remaining sound stitching. It's very tempting to have a go, because those neat readymade holes in the leather make it look as easy as a dot-to-dot children's sewing project. However, if you are really keen, you should get yourself a copy of a good leatherworking handbook to learn the basic techniques.

Right: Old leather belts and straps make smart binding for files and portfolios.

QUICK IDEAS FOR USING LEATHER SCRAPS

Soft leather is as useful as any other fabric for recycling into furnishing accessories, so don't discard damaged document cases or torn upholstery, and keep a lookout for oddments that could be put to practical use. Equip yourself with a pair of pinking shears or strong scissors and a heavy-duty hole puncher (from do-it-yourself shops) and you'll be able to add leather trimmings to all sorts of things.

Old belts and bag straps: These make instant curtain tie-backs complete with their own buckle fastenings. Or cut the leather into equal-length tabs and stitch them along the edge of a fabric panel to make a tab-top curtain. Use a leather belt as contrasting banding for pretty box files, or just snip off the two 'working' ends and glue them inside the front of the box and the lid so that it can be buckled shut like a picnic hamper.

Chamois leathers (and sound parts of disintegrating upholstery): Make these into little drawstring bags to store cutlery or jewellery, or to make gift bags for presents. Stitch two squares together around three sides, then turn the pouch inside out and punch a row of holes around the open end so that you can thread a cord or ribbon through them to close it. Or stitch several chamois leathers together to make a patchwork leather cushion cover.

Leather shoelaces: Use them in place of ribbons – for tying cushioned seat pads onto chair backs, for making tie-top curtains or for lashing together the fabric panels of director's chairs. Braid them or thread them with beads (knotting the ends together to keep the beads in place) and use them to tie around linen napkins. Or snip short pieces to make loop buttonholes as a smart fastening for cushions and covers.

Q What is the best way of looking after suede items?

A The matt finish and soft suppleness of suede never seem to go out of fashion, so you could come across anything from belts and document cases to cushions and suede-covered books. Suede is leather that has been split to expose the fibrous layer beneath the grained surface. But the distinctive textured finish can disappear if dirt is allowed to build up, turning it smooth and shiny. Sometimes brushing with a suede brush is enough to restore it, by fluffing up the surface again. But you may need to use a little white spirit (mineral spirits) first to tackle specific marks. Patch-test first for colour, then apply it with a cloth and finish with the brush. If it looks as though doing this will lift the colour, try rubbing grease spots with a pencil eraser instead.

---

presentation boxes

Look out for small leather presentation boxes, often sold second-hand without their contents. Usually lined with velvet or silk, these probably once held things like medals, pens, jewellery, watches, and sometimes scientific or medical instruments. They may be interesting purely because of their history, but some of them can be reused as gift boxes.

Q I enjoy buying old leather-bound books. Are they best kept on open shelves or in a glass-fronted bookcase? And is it possible to clean off any marks?

A The important thing with books is to get the humidity right, which generally means keeping them on open shelves to allow maximum ventilation all around them. Protecting them behind glass may reduce the amount of dirt they're exposed to (especially in a room where people smoke, for instance), but the reduction in ventilation can lead to mould and insect infestations, so you need to weigh up the risks. Your best option is probably to keep them on open shelves but check them annually for signs of damp or mould – especially if they are against external walls or near chimneys.

The most likely marks will be from grease caused by handling, and from damp. As long as the book isn't valuable, you could try cleaning grease marks with a little white spirit (mineral spirits), but test for colour fastness first, as though you're cleaning leather upholstery (see page 63). Water stains are more or less indelible – remember never to put a glass down on a book cover because you'll probably end up with a permanent ring mark.

Don't feel you ought to clean leather covers just for the sake of it. The dressings you can buy to treat leather are generally oil-based, and are no substitute for the humidity needed to keep it supple. If the atmosphere is too dry, the leather will dry out however much you try to 'feed' it. And if the atmosphere is too damp, the dressing can actually encourage mould growth – the mould may be able grow at a slightly lower humidity than usual because of the extra nutrients you're supplying. So be careful not to apply any cleaning products too generously or too often. It won't help preserve your book covers and it may darken the leather, especially if the surface is damaged.

---

gold tooling

Always be careful to avoid gold tooling when cleaning, waxing or staining leather.

Right: Old books need careful handling. Don't overclean leather covers or rub at gold tooling, and don't pull at the spines when removing them from shelves.

Q I've bought a writing desk with a leather inlay that is slightly worn and scuffed around the edges. Should I repair it or replace it completely?

A It's up to you. If it's a valuable desk you should consult a leather expert before taking any action. If not, there are a few simple steps you can take to improve the condition of the existing leather, or, if you want to replace it, it's a fairly straightforward job – and one you can tackle yourself.

To refix the original panel

The original leather is usually stuck down with a water-based adhesive, so you could use a good-quality paper glue. Restorers tend to use wheat starch, which is easily reversible in case you want to take it up again later and replace it. Where the leather is peeling up around the edges, lightly paste the top of the desk beneath it (this surface will be slightly recessed so that the leather sits flush with the wood). Now press the leather back into place and smooth it out carefully so that it butts up to the wood.

To tackle cracks and scratches

Dry or cracked leather can be revitalized with a lanolin and beeswax preparation available from specialist suppliers. (This may also help to ease any impressions left in the leather by writing with a ballpoint pen.) Once applied, the lanolin and beeswax should be left for 24 hours while the leather absorbs it. The surface can then be buffed gently with a soft, clean cloth. You may be able to touch up scratches by adopting a sort of French polishing technique if you can find a woodstain to match the leather. Ready-mixed wood stains in different colours can be thinned with solvent, then applied with a brush. Leave it to dry for four hours, then rub in a little beeswax and buff with a duster.

To fit a new panel

New leather panels in different colours are available, with the appropriate fixing instructions, from specialist suppliers, often by mail order. They will cut the leather to size (with a border to allow for trimming) and supply it complete with gold tooling. To fit it, you paste the indented area of the desk with a wallpaper adhesive, then carefully lay the new leather in place. Smooth it out with a cloth to get remove any wrinkles and air bubbles, then trim off the edges with a sharp craft knife so that it butts right up to the wood surround.

Q A stall in my local market always has dozens of quite small leather cases in different shapes and sizes. Although they look good, I never really know whether it's worth buying them, as I can't tell what most of them are used for.

A People used to be far better equipped for travelling than we are these days – with individual cases designed to carry every conceivable object. The objects themselves are often obsolete now, or beyond repair, but the cases stack up enticingly on flea market stalls. Half the enjoyment of collecting these is guessing what they were originally used for – and the other half is devising new functions for them.

Hat boxes

Round or oval cases, sometimes slightly scooped-out in shape, were originally designed to hold hats without crushing them. They're still useful for hats you only wear occasionally yet want to keep in good condition, and are also perfect for storing items like gloves, belts and scarves.

Music cases

These look like slim, flat briefcases with a flap-over top, usually fastened with a metal rod that slips over the handle, rather than a lock or buckle. They are just the right size for filing away documents or storing stationery, or even for using as small briefcases. Be careful not to overload them, though, as too much weight will drag on the handle and pull the case out of shape.

Binocular and camera cases

The shapes of these little buckled cases with shoulder straps vary from square to rounded (you can almost trace the development of camera design through them). Their neat size makes them incredibly practical, especially in a home office. Use the flat-shaped designs for postcards, envelopes, address labels and business cards. The rest make handy containers for desk essentials such as paperclips, staples and ink cartridges.

Above: Small cases designed to hold cameras or binoculars make handy storage for desk essentials.

Necessaires

These small travelling cases are often divided into separate compartments to hold toiletries, shaving equipment, hairbrushes and so on. They are perfect to hold sewing paraphernalia and a host of other essentials.

metal

e rely on metal so much in everyday life – for cooking, eating, digging the garden, locking the front door – that it's sometimes hard to recognize it as the same material that can create the wonderfully decorative effects of engraved silver or trompe l'oeil toleware. Few materials can reinvent themselves so completely. Second-hand metalwork lurks in flea markets and antiques shops in all its guises – turning up one day on a kitchenware stall, another among painted garden accessories, presenting itself as a gleaming and perfectly turned-out christening present, or hiding under layers of rust in an architectural salvage yard. You'll find bright copper, sober pewter, punched tin and colourful enamel – forgotten things left half-buried in the garden as well as perfect pieces in lovingly maintained condition. Each has its own place and needs different treatment. Some are easy to tackle at home, while others demand professional restoration work. It's difficult to become an expert in such a wide field, so you will probably have to choose a direction and stick with it. You will discover your own favourites as you seek out collectables, learning to recognize items with potential and devising innovative uses for them.

TRADITIONAL SILVER CLEANING TIPS

There are hundreds of traditional remedies for cleaning your silver. Try them with caution to see which suits you best.

○ Add 4 teaspoons salt and 4 teaspoons baking soda to 1 litre (35fl oz) water. Soak the silver for 10 minutes, then rinse thoroughly, dry carefully with a clean cloth and polish with a chamois leather.

○ Mix your own silver polish from 70g (2½oz) chalk powder (fine grains of limestone, or calcium carbonate), 85ml (3fl oz) household ammonia, 125ml (4fl oz) methylated spirit (denatured alcohol) and 500ml (18fl oz) water. Pour into a glass bottle, seal and shake before use.

○ Remove the tarnish from silver by wiping it with household ammonia and then polishing.

○ Immerse tarnished silver in buttermilk, then buff it up with a soft cloth.

Q I've bought a silver dressing table set – brush, comb and hand mirror – decorated with intricate engraving. What's the best way to clean it?

A The tarnish that develops on silver is caused by sulphur compounds in the atmosphere and by salt and grease deposits on the skin, so the more they are handled the more they will tarnish. The metal first acquires a pinkish tinge, then darkens to brown and ends up dark grey or black, without much shine left. The easiest way to remove tarnish is with one of the proprietary silver-cleaning cloths. As long as the tarnish is light and the surface smooth, this will produce a brightly polished finish (and a chemical contained in the cloth will help to prevent further tarnishing).

The trouble with engraved silver, though, is that a cloth won't be able to clean effectively inside the detail. Also, residues of cleaning product may become trapped in it, causing even more damage. (If you spot green deposits on the surface of sterling silver, for instance, it could be that the copper in the alloy is being corroded by

the residue of past cleaning materials.) To clean engraved and decorated surfaces effectively, you'll need to use a liquid or powder. Opinions differ on this. Some experts prefer liquid silver dip, and recommend that powders should only be used by specialist restorers. Others feel that silver dip tends to over-clean and to remove the bloom of the metal – and that it is more likely to leave a residue in the decoration. If you suspect your dressing table set may be valuable, it's worth consulting a professional on which method to use: otherwise, try out both with caution to see which you prefer.

Silver dip works by chemically dissolving the tarnish. Following the instructions on the container and wearing protective gloves, you either literally 'dip' the item in it (but don't let it stand, as you will end up with a tidemark), or apply it with cotton wool (absorbent cotton). It leaves a surface that will tarnish again quickly, so you need to finish by rinsing with water and drying thoroughly with a cotton cloth. And don't use dip if the silver is plate rather than sterling, as the strong chemical will gradually strip the

Above: Engraved silver needs careful cleaning to bring out the beauty of the decorated surface. You may need to use a special silver brush.

plating instead of just removing the tarnish (see page 76 for the distinction between plate and sterling silver).

Powder needs to be applied with a silver brush (like a big toothbrush with a long handle) which is stiff enough to remove the dry powder but not so stiff that it scratches the silver. Brush it off, then polish with a soft cloth. To clean the brush leave it in a saucer or shallow dish of bleach, but don't let the bleach touch the silver.

What all the experts agree on is that silver shouldn't be polished too hard or too often, or you will simply wear away its beauty and value. Specialist wadding and cream cleaners containing abrasives can be useful for tackling stubborn marks, but don't use them for regular cleaning. They could remove a thin layer of silver along with the tarnish, gradually wearing away any decoration and weakening the metal.

Q I've found a second-hand silver bowl that is very elegant but rather dented. Can I get it back into shape?

A Only if you're sure it's not of any particular value. Sometimes very thin silver is soft enough to be malleable, in which case you might be able to press out the dent with your fingers. But it's not like a hat – pushing the metal back into place will still leave an impression of the dent, and possibly of your fingers, too. Whatever you do, don't try to hammer it back into shape. If the piece is of any value, take it to a professional restorer. They may be able to help, or they may recommend that it be left as it is, dents and all. Signs of past use are part of the item's history and should add to your enjoyment of it, especially as they will contribute to the interest of the surface, adding shadows and variations in patina which will catch the light in different ways.

Q What's the difference between solid silver and silver plate, and how can I be sure what I'm buying?

A Judging silver is notoriously difficult, so don't feel too bad about your uncertainty. It's better to be cautious than over-confident – as long as you start with enough basic information to ask the right questions and check a few key points. Just bear in mind that there are few real bargains and it's easy to make mistakes.

You won't actually find anything made of 100 per cent silver, as it would be too soft to be of any practical use. 'Solid' is another term for 'sterling' silver, which is 92.5 per cent silver, the other 7.5 per cent being a harder metal, usually copper, to create a stronger alloy. Plate, on the other hand, is a sterling silver surface fused onto a less valuable metal. The technique was invented in the 18th century with Sheffield plate, in which sheets of copper were sandwiched between sheets of silver and then fashioned into different items. But it was superseded around 100 years later by the electroplating process, which allowed already crafted metal items to be given a coating of pure silver by passing an electrical current through a bath of silver and potassium cyanide. Victorian plate is very collectable as long as it's in good condition – and it's also about a quarter of the price of sterling silver dating from the same period.

Each type has its own form of hallmark, and if you're keen on collecting silver seriously you need to learn to recognize and interpret these accurately. It's all too easy for novices to be misled by forged or adapted marks – besides which, some genuine pieces won't be marked at all. In general, British sterling will have a hallmark representing the city of manufacture, the maker and the date, and incorporating an 'assay' mark (a lion passant, or walking) to prove that the purity of the metal has been tested. The marking of Sheffield plate varied, sometimes incorporating a crown, or the words 'best Sheffield heavy silver plating', but many pieces of Sheffield plate were unmarked. Electroplated silver will usually be marked 'EPNS' (electroplated nickel silver) plus 'A1' to denote the best quality.

❍ As well as getting to know the hallmarks, try to get a feel for the silver itself, looking out for thinness in the metal where the hallmark (or another inscription) may have been removed, or a change in the patina where it has been patched over or altered.

❍ With old Sheffield plate, look out for places where the underlying copper has worn through the silver. You sometimes find this in more elaborate designs where solid silver ornament was soldered onto the main piece: if the joins became weakened they exposed the base metal and left jagged edges or unpolishable surfaces.

❍ It's always easy to find old cutlery in flea markets – appealingly beribboned bundles as well as individual ladles and serving spoons. They're usually temptingly inexpensive (and make great presents if you repackage them in a smart box or velvet pouch) but always ask to undo the ties and check individual pieces. See if they're a matching set, check them for the A1 quality mark and avoid cutlery with worn plating, where the underlying copper shows through. It may have been eroded over the years by abrasive cleaning or dishwasher detergents, and the cost of replating will probably outweigh the value of your bargain.

❍ The electroplated finish is brighter than either sterling or Sheffield plate, because of the pure silver content, but it will tarnish more easily, especially if used for foods such as brassica vegetables, salt and eggs (egg spoons always need special attention), so you need to clean items immediately after using them. Items like soup spoons and fish knives that aren't brought out so often will stay brighter, but with everyday pieces make sure each item in the set gets equal use so that they age and wear evenly.

❍ Don't be tempted to cram silver cutlery into a dishwasher as the pieces will scratch each other – load each section of the compartment with just a handful of pieces.

Below: Get to know the difference between sterling silver and plate, and learn to recognize authentic hallmarks.

Q I've bought an old tray with a very pretty painted design that is spotted by rust in places – can the surface be repaired?

A Yes, although it will be probably be difficult to disguise the fact that some parts are newer than others. It rather depends on the style of the design and the amount of damage. Something fairly bold like bargeware (the flamboyantly painted pieces traditionally used on canal boats) will take retouching without the new paintwork being too obvious. On more delicate items such as toleware, however, any heavy-handed brushwork and mismatched colours will be more difficult to hide. Toleware covers various kinds of decorated tin – including découpage, painting and lacquerwork. These sometimes had a subtle trompe l'oeil finish, creating the effect of other surfaces such as wood, leather or tortoiseshell, which would need the skills of a paint-effects expert to restore.

Tackle the rust spots first. A traditional rust-removal remedy is 1 tablespoon of citric acid mixed with 500ml (18fl oz) water. Because this mixture could remove some of the design along with the rust, test a sample area first. Assuming the design is not affected, brush the corroded spots gently with this solution to remove the crusted surface, still proceeding with caution, then rinse and dry thoroughly.

The original tray would probably have been painted with something like lampblack and shellac, which is difficult to recreate exactly with modern products. To repair the design, however, you could try the tiny pots of coloured lacquer used for painting models (found in hobby shops and catalogues).

However carefully you work, you will still find that the new paintwork stands out as brighter and shinier than the old. The only way to blend old and new effectively is to add a coat of varnish over the top of the whole thing to unify the surface, and then rub it back gently with fine steel wool to take off the shine.

Q I occasionally come across old enamel storage jars – are they still usable?

A Yes, as long as you check their condition and line them if necessary before using them for foodstuffs. Enamelware first appeared at the end of the 19th century, providing practical, economical containers for domestic kitchens, laundries and bathrooms. Its practical nature is immortalized in the plain, functional items familiar from mid-20th-century camping and picnicware, but many of the earlier pieces were far more decorative and colourful, especially the European designs. Pretty floral patterns and bold Art Deco geometrics made enamel every bit as design-conscious as china, while Dutch pieces were usually patterned with blue-and-white images inspired by traditional delftware. Red, blue and white are the most common colours, but you might occasionally come across yellow or green, and even pink or mauve. Avoid white enamel with painted decoration that looks as though it isn't the right age or style: you'll probably find that it was added later, and it will spoil the authenticity of the piece.

Complete sets of storage canisters were made for kitchens, often labelled with their intended contents – flour, rice, sugar and so on – in French or English, depending on the country of origin. Individual utility items included saucepans and jugs, matchbox holders and spoon or ladle racks, along with soap dishes, pitchers and washbasins designed for bathrooms.

Because this was in constant use, it tended to acquire chips and dents, and sets rarely survived intact. You are therefore more likely to find odd pieces than complete sets, but they are still attractive. In fact, the occasional chip will help to keep the price down without detracting seriously from the overall appeal of the design. Don't attempt to retouch the enamel colour, but be careful not to use damaged pieces in which to cook, serve or store food, as rust can develop on the exposed metal beneath. Line containers with plastic bags first and keep old jugs for decorative use rather than serving drinks. To prevent further

damage, it's best to wash your enamelware by hand and dry it thoroughly to discourage rust. And if you're worried that a particular piece just isn't good enough for kitchen use, keep it for plants and flowers: it's bound to find a practical home in the garden or on a window-sill.

Above: Traditional enamelware makes a colourful display on kitchen shelves, but you should line damaged interiors before using it to store foodstuffs.

Q I seem to have acquired quite a collection of traditional tin kitchenware, without any idea of what to do with these pieces. Are they just nostalgia items or can I put them to practical use?

A Something about the intriguing shapes and simple mechanics of old-fashioned cooking accoutrements makes them irresistibly collectable. Childhood memories of helping out in the kitchen – mixing cake batter, cutting pastry shapes and icing cookies – are partly responsible. But it's also probably because all those pastry cutters and jelly moulds represent a slice of history from the lives of the well-prepared cooks and housewives who used them. In fact, this still holds true even if you are too young to remember kitchens equipped with anything more traditional than all-in-one food processors. The manufacturing techniques and materials may have evolved further, but many of the designs have barely changed since the 19th century, when baking trays, graters and colanders were mass-produced for Victorian households. And the decorative moulds that helped keep up appearances at the dinner table by turning out flawless jellies, mousses and ice cream represent a classic snapshot of upstairs-downstairs life.

Many keen cooks today enjoy having original kitchenware as part of their batterie de cuisine. In the first place, there is the sheer practical simplicity of classic cake tins, not to mention the intriguing possibilities of less familiar items such as hinged double-sided ice-cream moulds designed to turn out perfect fruit shapes. Also, a display of ladles, sieves, graters, whisks, infusers and so on, hung on butcher's hooks above the worktop, will create interesting shapes against the wall. And even if your culinary skills are fairly basic, there are plenty of ways to put these functional items to decorative use.

❍ Pastry cutters are brilliant devices for shaping decorative stamps to print your own designs on paper and fabric. Use a cut potato as your base: push the cutter into the potato, then cut away the

excess potato from around the cutter. Now pull it away so that you are left with a clearly outlined stamp shape with a chunky potato 'handle'.

❍ Colanders make excellent fruit bowls.

❍ Use the most interesting-shaped cutters to make hanging mobiles or Christmas tree decorations. String shapes together across a window, hang them from a light fitting or tie them to the tree with colourful ribbons. You could even spray them gold or silver if they're too well-used to look celebratory.

Above: Old kitchenware has a dozen practical uses –
cake tins make neat office trays for essentials such as
paperclips and drawing pins.

❍ French tin brioche moulds and madeleine tins
are perfect candle holders: sit a tealight or pillar
candle in each one.

❍ Graters create instant lanterns: stand a candle
inside so that the light twinkles through the cut
holes in the tin.

LOOKING AFTER KITCHEN COPPER

Kitchen moulds, as well as saucepans and mixing
bowls, were traditionally made of copper – the
metal is an excellent heat conductor and many
professional cooks and chefs believe it provides the
best surface for whisking egg whites. Modern
copper is lined with steel as a protective coating,
but old copper items may suffer from tarnish or
verdigris.

❍ To remove tarnish, rub with half a lemon dipped
in salt.

❍ To add an extra shine to copper items, polish
them with a cloth dipped in vinegar and sprinkled
with a little salt.

❍ Verdigris, which develops through contact with
acid and fat, is poisonous if consumed, so it must
be removed before the copper is used to prepare
food. The traditional way of removing it is to use
a solution of salt and ammonia: mix ½ teaspoon of
salt and a dash of household ammonia in 250 ml
(1 cup) of water. Wearing rubber gloves, use it on
a cloth to wipe off the verdigris, then polish with a
clean cloth and chalk powder (fine grains of
limestone, or calcium carbonate).

Q I've bought an old meat safe, but the wire front is coming away. What's the best way to replace it?

A Meat safes were the traditional way of keeping food cool and ventilated but protected from flies. These small cupboards with a fine mesh front are somewhat superfluous now that refrigerators do the job for us, but they are a useful size so it's worth finding another role for them if you can. A punched-tin panel, as you'd find on an Early American pie safe, will make a prettier door front than the old mesh, so pull the remains of the mesh away and concentrate on transforming a utilitarian object into a decorative piece.

To make a punched-tin panel

1 Sand and paint the cupboard with emulsion (latex) or eggshell to create a matt or low-sheen surface, then cut a sheet of tin-plated metal about 1.5cm (⅝in) larger all around than the space left for it.

2 Plan the design you are going to punch out and carefully draw it to scale on a sheet of paper – it could be a simple geometric pattern such as a diamond shape, a Shaker-style heart, a date to commemorate a special occasion or perhaps lettering to spell out the contents of the cupboard.

3 Lay the metal panel on a wooden board and tape your design securely in place. Now punch out the pattern with a hammer and nail, working along the line of your sketch and leaving a small space between each punch hole. (Be careful not to punch them too close together or they may run into one another and leave a split in the metal instead of a hole.)

4 Buff the panel with steel wool and clean it with a cloth dipped in white spirit (mineral spirits). To age the surface and make it more in keeping with

Left: An old meat safe, restored with a smart new punched-tin front, makes a neat cupboard for storing kitchen crockery.

the cupboard, paint on a patinating fluid (from art and craft shops). Wear gloves and goggles, as this is toxic. Then wipe with jade oil (from hardware and paint shops), which 'dries' metal and retards tarnishing.

5 Attach the metal panel to the inside of the cupboard door with galvanized nails, then nail wooden battens around each side to cover the rough edges.

Q What's the best way of cleaning and caring for old pewter?

A The appeal of pewter is its workaday, down-to-earth look and classless style. By the middle of the 16th century it was standard household ware in Europe – everyone used it, rich or poor. Because it tended to be traded in when old or damaged, there are very few really old pieces around – if you find an olde-worlde lidded tankard or pair of baronial candlesticks, they're unlikely to be authentic. Pewter got a new lease of life at the start of the 20th century, when the London store Liberty began selling decorative pieces made from pewter. It continued to flourish in the 1920s and '30s when it was used to create distinctive Art Deco pieces, as well as reproductions of older designs.

The traditional unpolished finish that we associate with pewter items – subdued and unpretentious – is part of its history. In fact, it starts off polished and that distinctive patina develops with wear after about 50 years. But the muted surface should still have a soft gleam, which is one way of telling the difference between old and new. Some modern reproduction pewter has a simulated patina that dulls the metal but doesn't glow as it should. The shine can be restored to contemporary pieces with a duster and metal polish, but older pewter should simply be washed now and then in hot water with mild detergent. Never try to remove any darker patina: you'll be taking off the surface of the metal itself.

Q I'd like to install an old enamel bath in my bathroom. What should I check before I buy?

A An old roll-top bath with its traditional claw feet has tremendous style as long as you have a big enough room to take it. (The idea of a free-standing bath is that it really should be free-standing, so don't try to cram one in where there isn't space.) Original designs will be made of cast iron, and although modern pressed-steel copies are still being made, many people prefer the idea of preserving a bit of history.

Check the condition of the enamel first. Cast-iron baths produced by factory kiln-firing have a vitreous enamel finish that can't really be recreated once it's damaged, except at vast expense. Professional resurfacing companies can help restore some of the finish, treating the bath with a chemical bond and an enamel spray and then buffing it with an electric polisher. But it's better if you can find one that's in a condition you're happy to stick with. (If you do decide to have your bath professionally resurfaced, check out several potential restorers, ask for references and follow them up to make sure you're happy with their previous work. They will come to your home and complete the job on site.)

Now look at the feet. Claw feet are made separately and then bolted into place when the bath is installed. If you're buying second-hand, the feet may still be attached – but if they're supplied loose, check them carefully, as you need to make sure they fit properly. Sometimes the pair from the plughole end will be slightly shorter than the other pair, which is fine, but it's important that each is an exact pair so that the bath will stand steady on the floor.

There will probably be limescale stains to deal with (especially around the plughole and beneath the taps), and possibly rust. You may find you can remove the limescale with a cut lemon (which is acidic enough to attack the calcium deposits, but if it is too old and stubborn, use a proprietary cleaner. Rust can be tackled by a rust remover. (Don't worry if you spot rust marks inside the bath: it won't be eating its way through from the outside, but is more likely the result of another item having been stacked in it at the salvage yard.) Prime the outside with a metal primer and paint with a low-sheen eggshell finish.

---

buying old taps

Make sure that the taps have been 're-seated' so that the water flow isn't affected by a build-up of limescale inside the tap. Unscrew the body and wheelhead and feel inside. If it feels encrusted or corroded, this needs be dealt with to prevent the tap from dripping when it should be closed, and trickling when it should be open. Avoid oversized taps – they look good but are invariably difficult to install and maintain, because washers have to be specially cut for them.

Q How can I restore a 1940s mirrored bathroom cabinet which is smothered in grungey layers of paint?

A These cabinets are usually made of tin, a soft metal with high 'scratchability' needing gentle handling. First protect the mirror with masking tape and a sheet of newspaper. Then apply proprietary paint remover to one section at a time. Allow the chemical to blister the paint but don't let it dry completely: instead removed the softened paint with a paint scraper (avoiding heavy pressure or scratching) or with fine wire wool. For a shiny, modern effect, repeat until all layers of paint are removed. If you prefer an aged, distressed look, leave patches of the bottom paint layers in place. Then clean the cabinet with a soft cloth dipped in white spirit and let it dry.

Right: Old roll-top baths and traditional taps recreate a sense of authentic style in country bathrooms.

Q I've bought a set of second-hand metal garden furniture – not old but quite a pretty shape. Can I repaint it?

A Garden furniture – even the mass-produced pieces churned out today – tends to be designed along fairly traditional lines, so you'll often find modern cast-aluminium furniture in pretty, café-style shapes. Of course, the telltale parasol hole in the middle of the table will remind you that they were made in the age of convenience, but the advantage of this is that they also have a tough, weatherproof factory finish that makes them easy to maintain. What you may want to do, however, is paint over the shiny white or ubiquitous green that are the two shades most metal garden furniture comes in now. This finish is probably a cellulose paint, so you'll need a cellulose-based undercoat before you can add your top colour. Make sure the shade you choose for your undercoat is lighter than the colour you're going to use on top. If the existing base is dark, it's better to cover it with a couple of layers of pale undercoat than with a single dark coat that will then need numerous top coats. For a subtle finish, use something like exterior eggshell, which is weatherproof but gives a mellow, matt surface.

Bare metal furniture – perhaps a decorative table designed for indoor use – can be painted for the garden, too. You'll need to use a metal primer, then undercoat, then finish with exterior eggshell. Remember to paint the underneath of chair and table feet, as well as the visible parts, so that they don't leave rust marks on your paving when you move them. It's generally best to store the furniture indoors over winter. If you have traditional slatted folding chairs, it's a good idea to treat the joints with grease or lubricant spray when you bring them in, so that they don't seize up while out of use.

Q I love the look of old garden buckets and watering cans, but are they usable?

A You need to check them before you buy, to make sure they're watertight for the garden. The easiest way to do this is to hold them up to the light – rust holes and splits will be clearly visible. Also look to see if they've been mended in the past: you'll sometimes find them plugged with makeshift repairs made from things like pennies wedged in with putty. Of course, this adds to their history and you may enjoy them as part of a collection, but they're not practical.

If a bucket already has holes, that's just the start: it means the galvanized surface that makes it rustproof has been breached and it will gradually get worse. Check how the can or bucket sits, too. If it's not flat on the ground, you've got problems. It has probably been left outside in cold weather with water standing in it, which will have frozen and expanded, blowing out the bottom of the container. Once this has happened the metal is weakened and can easily start to leak.

Old painted buckets and watering cans are particularly nice, and very collectable – in the end, it doesn't really matter whether or not they're watertight as you're more likely to keep them for an indoor display.

---

cleaning guidelines

When cleaning and restoring metal artefacts, always lay them on protective newspaper and a soft cloth to avoid damaging your work surface. Avoid using abrasives or steel wool to polish soft metals like aluminium or brass, which are easily scratched. Don't try to remove the attractive brown or green patina on bronze as this adds to its charm and value.

Right: Traditional painted watering cans can be used for decoration or display if they're no longer robust enough for practical garden work.

Q I like the look of old metal-framed beds, but how easy are they to restore for use?

A Metal bedframes can conjure up several different looks – the neat institutional order of school dormitories, the polished bedknobs of Victorian Christmas cards or the pretty, decorative effects of French country style. When you find them in second-hand shops and antiques markets, however, they're likely to have been dismantled and stacked in a bundle of flat pieces – head, foot, side struts and so on. The most important thing to check is that all the pieces are there so that the bed can be reassembled properly. In particular, make sure the side struts are equal lengths and come from the same bed. Sometimes they may come with a separate metal-link base that slots into the frame; sometimes the bed may have a central base joining head and foot pieces rather than central side shafts; but sometimes there may not be a base at all and you will have to create one from wooden slats, or use the frame with a divan base (see below).

You may find that you can use the frames as a decorative addition to an existing bed, either by slotting a basic divan inside it or by fixing wrought-iron head and foot pieces to a modern base. If you're lucky enough to come across an old French daybed – designed with high end pieces, rather like a child's cot – you could fit it with a foam cushion base rather than a mattress and use it as a sofa or garden seat.

Check the height before you commit yourself. Beds from schools, hospitals and army barracks are often unexpectedly high, making them not suitable for small children and not practical for low-ceilinged rooms. It's easy to misjudge dimensions when you're looking at furniture in the setting of a cavernous auction showroom, so take measurements carefully and think about how

Left: Traditional metal-framed beds look perfect in children's rooms, and can be painted to create a lighter, prettier effect.

well it will fit the room it's destined for. Also bear in mind that these frames are very heavy and the metal feet will dig into your carpets. Try to find metal caster cups to protect them (Bakelite ones will crack).

Distressed paintwork is part of the appeal of these beds, but if you want to change the colour, or you're concerned that it might contain lead, just rub off any loose, flaking paint and recoat with eggshell.

---

mattresses

Don't expect the beds to come complete with mattresses; you'll need to buy new ones to fit. This may not be easy, because old beds – particularly if they've come from French markets, as many of them have – will probably not have been made to standard modern widths. However, there are specialist companies that will make traditional ticking mattresses to order (see pages 148-156).

---

adapting furniture and fittings

As well as furniture and recognisable fittings, look out for metal items that can be adapted to other domestic uses.

○ Traditional flat-irons, which make useful doorstops and paperweights.

○ Old advertising or direction signs – particularly good as alternative pictures for teenagers' rooms.

○ Cast-iron manhole covers. These provide unusual firebacks for open fireplaces. Purpose-made firebacks – even reproduction designs – can be very expensive, so this is an excellent alternative. You'll need a large fireplace to take a full-size square or rectangular cover, but circular coal-hole lids will fit smaller fireplaces.

Q My local flea market often sells old door hardware and architectural details – handles, latches, knockers, boot scrapers and so on. Can they be cleaned up for use?

A Definitely. You just need to remove surface rust and then oil or varnish them to protect the surface.

Old letterboxes and door knockers are sometimes coated with generations of paint. To strip this off, put the items in a plastic bucket with caustic soda dissolved in cold water in the proportions recommended on the packaging. Always wear rubber gloves and work in a well-ventilated area or in the open air because of the fumes. Make sure each piece is attached to a wire so that you can fish it out of the bucket to check its progress. Scrub or hose off the loose paint with clean water, and continue until the stripping is complete. You can then prime the items with a metal primer and repaint: use a black or near-black exterior eggshell for a traditional cast-iron effect. Alternatively, you could oil them with teak or tung oil for a warm, glowing finish. Or varnish with two or three coats of matt or satin varnish to seal the metal, then rub it back with fine-grade steel wool and add wax polish for a soft pewter-like glow.

Door handles will usually need to be bought in pairs complete with the square shaft that links them. You'll also find individual knobs or pulls designed to be used on external doors. On Georgian or Victorian front doors these were usually fixed centrally, but they also make elegant curtain hold-backs if you set them on either side of a window. The other thing to look out for is lever handles, particularly wrought-iron designs from windows and French doors. Even if the spindles or other 'workings' are missing, these can be used as pull handles on cupboard doors – or, again, fitted next to a window so that curtains can be hooked behind them.

Old locks and keys, which are often far more ornamental than the modern equivalents, can be renovated and reinstated by specialist locksmiths, who will re-oil locks and also cut new keys to fit.

Big keys with decorative heads can be trimmed with tassels for use in dressing tables and on bedroom doors.

Also look out for decorative railing heads, finials from conservatory roofs and metal pelmets from verandas and summerhouses. You may not have the conservatory or summerhouse to put them to their original use, but their ornamental shapes are a shame to waste. Place them along the edges of paths and flowerbeds, or just keep them for display on shelves and window-sills.

Q How do I restore a set of rusty kitchen scales, which seem to be made of several different metals?

A Some metals accept more aggressive cleaning that others, so your first step is to identify what you're dealing with. The main body of scales is usually cast iron with steel workings, and bowls in brass or tin.

1 Remove any rust on cast iron and steel surfaces with a commercial product (or paint on liquid paraffin to soften it, then leave for a few hours and rub off with fine steel wool). Clean the surfaces with a soft cloth dipped in white spirit and towel dry.
2 Tackle fine scratches with a layer of polish. Deeper scratches can be rubbed away with fine emery paper, or with a paste of whiting mixed with methylated spirits or paraffin. Finish with a coat of liquid wax to protect against further rust.
3 Clean brass parts with a commercial metal polish and paint with clear varnish to prevent tarnishing. Don't over-clean the weights: these are usually untreated brass, lead or steel and excess cleaning could affect the exact measures.

Right: Flea markets are usually a good source of traditional door handles and other details that can be restored to practical use.

stone

Stone is the most traditional of domestic materials, creating a natural link between the house and the garden, and capable of conjuring up both classical elegance and rustic simplicity. It's often thought of as cold, and doesn't immediately suggest much sense of colour, but in fact it embraces a wide range of shades and effects, from the golden warmth of York stone to the fine veining of delicately coloured marble.

Your most likely stone finds will be decorative statuary and garden containers – often relatively new, and not necessarily hand-crafted. Don't disregard them: their modern surfaces can easily be mellowed and worked comfortably into an older setting. But the real pleasure will come from authentic architectural details that reflect the structure of the traditional home. The stone spheres on its gateposts, the flags laid in its hallway and the carved corbels that once supported a heavy arch or lintel all carry a history with them. Old stone awakens the market-browser's delight in uncovering the secrets of the past, camouflaged by years of wear and weathering. You can preserve that patina and enjoy the sense of age it represents, or clean off the layers to see what lies beneath. Either course will bring its own rewards.

Q How can I make use of a slab of marble, originally from an old bathroom washstand?

A Assuming that it's a complete length – without the hole that is sometimes cut into these tops to hold the wash basin – you have several options. Do check first, though, that it really is marble. Consider the weight: if it feels too light for its size, then you may have a piece of stone dressed up to look like marble. Also check the underside where it was fixed to the washstand. If the newly exposed section is plain white, without any veining, then it's probably fake.

Marble is an attractive surface for both bedrooms and bathrooms, especially if it is veined in soft colours rather than anything too dark or heavy. If you like the idea of a traditional washstand, you could add your marble top to an existing cabinet or chest of drawers to recreate its original function. Be careful how you clean it: strong chemical cleaners or acidic substances will eat into the surface, so use only plain water.

The other obvious place to use marble is in the kitchen, where its coolness has distinct advantages. You could either use your slab to create a cool shelf in a pantry, or build it into the kitchen worktop where it will provide an ideal pastry-board – marble is the traditional surface on which to roll out pastry. Remember that it will be at risk from acidic substances, though, and will mark easily if, for instance, you try cutting fruit on it. Lemon juice on dark marble will quickly leave white streaks as the calcium is attacked by acid (that's why lemon juice is so good for removing limescale deposits from sinks and baths).

Left: Marble is an attractive, cool surface for bathrooms and kitchens. If you can't find a complete washstand, you may come across the marble top alone, which could be put to other use.

---

black marble

Watch out for black marble masquerading as slate. The two can be difficult to tell apart, but you'll soon find out if you install marble as a kitchen worktop, because the surface will mark and streak.

Q I've occasionally come across stone tablets carved with house names and dates from previous centuries, presumably from buildings that have since been demolished. How could I display one of these in a less ancient house without feeling a complete fraud?

A Display is the key word here. As long as you don't try to give the impression that the carving was part of the original house, you can't be accused of fraud. Think of it as a decorative plaque that can be hung above a fireplace or propped on a mantelpiece. (You might even find an old, disused gravestone, and as long as you don't feel uncomfortable about exploiting the life of a complete stranger, this would make a very striking garden feature.)

But why are you so squeamish about installing your stonework more permanently? There's no law against mixing furnishings and fittings from different periods. Houses continue to evolve and acquire new characteristics – it's what gives each one its individuality, and unless you are a purist in matters of architectural authenticity, there's no reason to worry about this natural progress. Try incorporating it into a kitchen worktop or tiled splashback. Or use it as the base for a small hearth: it will be obscured by ash in winter months, but will give the fireplace extra decoration in summer so that you don't need to worry about filling the grate with pinecones and dried flowers.

Above: Elegant stone architectural details, such as pieces from old gateposts, provide interesting sculptural shapes to set in a garden.

Q I've bought a box of stone architectural details. Some are very beautiful, but rather too ornate for my house. Any ideas for using them discreetly?

A The difficulty with architectural decoration is that it needs to suit the proportions of the room in which it's to be used. An elaborate ceiling rose will look out of place in a low-ceilinged country cottage. Similarly, classical cornicing will be too much for a simple setting.

As well as accentuating any less-than-perfectly-straight walls, it will add unnecessary clutter to a plain whitewashed wall. Individual smaller pieces can be put to effective use, however, and if you have a few well-carved stone corbels in your box, you are fortunate.

Corbels are essentially devices of support, used like brackets to hold up the ends of archways or mantelpieces. Sometimes you'll see them added purely for ornament, but the design is the same. If you can find a way of fixing them to the wall, they make perfect display shelves for individual items such as a vase or clock. But their right-angled shape makes them ideal for other practical purposes. Turn them upside down, so that the top surface acts as a base and the decorative carving is more visible, and you have a very elegant doorstop or – if you use them in pairs – an instant set of bookends.

Q How can I clean a batch of old stone flags, and should they be sealed before I put them to use?

A Stone flags can sometimes be found in architectural salvage yards, usually discoloured by years of use and grime. Their natural colour will vary according to where they came from originally – it could be anything from grey to yellow to green to brown, and you won't find out until you've cleaned them up. If you're feeling particularly energetic, you could get down on your knees and scrub them with paint stripper. But the easiest method is to tackle them with a good-quality pressure hosepipe and plenty of clean water.

Your stone flags can be laid as a floor indoors or out, and there isn't really any need to seal it. In fact, sealing can be a disadvantage as it will trap damp, which can then seep out as crystalline salts. Even worse, damp could work itself out sideways to penetrate the walls and cause further damage. But you will have to accept, if you leave the flags unsealed, that their absorbent surface will be hard to protect against liquids spilt on them. If you can't live with the thought of marks caused by oil or other stains, the only answer is don't lay a stone floor in a kitchen.

When you do need to remove marks, the best way to tackle them is with wet-and-dry sandpaper. This is available in packs of varying grades, and because you use it damp it won't create any dust. Work on the mark using the finest grade first, progressing to a harsher grade if you feel you need to.

Q Can I install an old stone scullery sink in my kitchen or utility room? What steps should I take to restore it?

A Your first step is to clean it up so that you can assess its condition more accurately. Don't use anything too harsh – a strong chemical cleaner or an acidic liquid such as vinegar could attack the surface of marble or limestone, so be cautious until you've established what the stone is. Try a very mild solution of washing-up liquid, specialist stone soap or a specialist cleaning product recommended by a stone retailer or tile shop, and don't scrub too hard.

Once it's clean, make a thorough check for cracks to ensure that the sink is usable. If you find that it's not, cut your losses at this stage and consign it to the garden as a plant container: there's nothing you can do to repair a cracked sink. Otherwise, you can go ahead with installing it. Consider the size when deciding where to put it. Many old stone sinks are quite shallow: you'll still find this shape in some traditional Mediterranean homes, but it's not the most practical shape for a modern kitchen. In this case you'd be better off fitting it in a utility room, where it would be perfect for helping you out with gardening and flower arranging.

Taps for this type of sink should be in traditional style. It's unlikely that they'll come as part of the deal, but you should be able to buy restored originals separately. Make sure that these comply with local water regulations before you plumb them in.

Q I've found a nice garden urn. From its bargain price, I'm presuming it's a mass-produced design rather than anything special, but the classic shape is very attractive. How can I make it look more authentic?

A It's worth checking first to make sure that it is only a moulded copy. The chances are that you're right and it's made of reconstituted stone (sand mixed with cement and poured into a mould) but original marble statuary is often sold off unexpectedly cheap because the seller doesn't realize that it's the real thing. It can be surprisingly difficult to tell the difference, but there are two key things you can check:

❍ First, gently scratch the urn to see if grains of sand come away from the surface. If they do, it's almost certainly reconstituted stone. But if they don't, it's just possible that you're dealing with marble. Marble left outside in the elements acquires a sugary, crystalline surface as the acid in the atmosphere attacks the calcium in the stone, so that it ends up looking like sandstone. (Many churchyards are full of old gravestones that look like sandstone but are actually 19th- or early 20th-century white marble that has lost its sleek surface.)

❍ The other trick is to check a part of the urn that hasn't been exposed – the base of the pedestal is an obvious place. If the piece is marble, this is where it should still look like it, because it's been protected from corrosion.

And if it turns out to be reconstituted stone after all, don't be disappointed. As you say, it's the shape that matters, and reconstituted stone actually ages rather well. It will stand up to the elements, because it's not affected by the pollutants in the air – but it will pick up lichens naturally because of its absorbency, so there's no need for you to age it artificially.

Q I couldn't resist a job lot of old red bricks that were going cheap – but what's the best way to use them in my garden?

A Patterns of traditional brick create beautiful floors and walkways among garden greenery. They are also practical to have underfoot, as the finish of the bricks themselves and the ridges formed by their edges ensure a textured, non-slip surface. But if you're thinking of laying them as a path or terrace, the most important thing is to check that they're frostproof. A quick check is to twist a coin into the surface really hard; if it doesn't cause any flaking or leave a mark, the brick is probably hard enough. But a better test is to leave a few bricks outside over the winter to see how they weather it. However much of a bargain they were to buy, it would be a complete waste of time and money to lay them now and then find they've cracked or crumbled after the first year.

As your supply of bricks is limited, you also need to plan your design carefully, calculating exactly how they will lie so that you can be sure that you have enough. Traditional herringbone patterns always look elegant, in both formal and cottage-style gardens, but you can also lay the bricks in a single direction, or alternate the direction to form a basketweave pattern. Circles or lozenge shapes can be incorporated in a plain design to accent specific features such as statuary, or – if you want to make the bricks go farther – you might want to use them as edging for a herb garden or gravel parterre. They can be laid either flat or on edge (assuming there are no holes or indentations in the sides).

Bear in mind that if you have the bricks laid professionally, you'll end up paying far more than the cost of the bricks. And even if you're planning on doing it yourself, it's worth estimating the cost of your time, because this is a fairly advanced project: they need to be either laid on a bed of mortar over hardcore and then pointed, or laid on a semi-dry mix of sand and cement, with dry mortar then brushed into the joints.

Create a brick hearth

If your supply of bricks won't stretch to an entire garden path, or their quality isn't consistent enough to create an even surface, an alternative option is to use them as a fireplace hearth. Lay them in a rectangle so that they act as a base for a free-standing grate and allow air to circulate beneath it.

Below: Old bricks — as long as they are frost-proof — can be laid in a variety of patterns to create garden paths and terrace floors.

rough or smooth

Always make sure the stone you are planning to use is appropriate for the purpose. Any stone intended for surfaces such as paths or steps needs to be slip-resistant – marble, for instance, isn't suitable for this purpose as the algae that develops on the surface will turn it into an ice rink in wet weather. Stone with a rough texture is likely to be far safer than smooth stone.

Q I'd like to renovate an old marble fireplace surround. How should I deal with any cracks, scratches or discoloration?

A Serious scratches and discoloration in marble will need expert attention. Professional restorers use hand-polishing techniques and special products or poultices to tackle the damage. There's not much that can be done about major cracks, but you could try filling smaller ones with epoxy resin. Test a small, unnoticeable area first to see the effect, and tint the resin with artist's powder pigment to match the colour of the marble.

If the marble has been painted over, it's worth getting an expert to check it out before you charge in and strip it back. There's a good chance that the painting was done to disguise a damaged surface, so you may find you're in for a lot more restoration work once you remove it.

Marble stains easily, and marks really need to be removed quickly, before they have a chance to 'take'. But the following remedies may help lift older marks.

❍ Rub with a cut lemon, making sure you wipe the juice away quickly before it eats into the marble itself.

❍ To remove smoke damage or other badly disfiguring marks, rub gently with a mixture of powdered pumice and water.

❍ To remove red wine stains, add a few drops of household ammonia to a solution of lemon juice.

❍ If the marble is matt, sprinkle stains with powdered pumice, add a few drops of vegetable oil, leave for few hours then rub off with a cloth.

Left: Classic marble fireplaces have a distinctive elegance that provides a natural background for other traditional artefacts. The surface can be restored by careful cleaning and maintenance.

Q I have just finished laying a terrace made from old flagstones, and have a couple of them left over. I don't want to waste them – could I turn them into a garden bench or table?

A If they're exactly the right size and shape, go ahead. You should be able to buy readymade pedestals – the sort designed to support statuary or containers – from a garden centre. As long as these are strong enough to take the weight of the stone slab, you can create your own bench by positioning one at each end, or, for a wider slab, one at each corner. (Even if you're not sure enough of the stability to use it as a seat, you can weight it with a row of container plants and use it as a shelf against an outdoor wall.) Alternatively, you might use sturdy lengths of log for a more rustic effect. One other option, for a smaller piece of stone, might be to use it as a plaque and have it professionally engraved with a house name or quotation (see pages 148-156). Granite or slate will provide the most durable surface, but sandstone or limestone will age with a more mellow finish.

If you can't think of a decorative purpose, remember that spare flagstones always come in handy as bases for statuary, planted containers and even barbecue grills. Don't feel you have to find a practical use for yours if the pieces you're left with don't suggest themselves for an obvious purpose. It may seem a shame to leave them unused, but your local stone merchant will have a huge stock of scraps, so you're almost guaranteed to find the size and shape you want. Chipped stone is of no value to the merchant, so stone that has been damaged during manufacture or transport will be dumped and can be picked up virtually free by anyone with the patience and stamina to sort through the dump. You'll need to wear old clothes and be prepared for a fair bit of rummaging, but you'll probably find that you are able to load up your car for relatively little expense. Just don't bother the merchants with queries – they'll expect you to get on with your search unaided.

Q I've bought a very useful stone column that would be ideal for a birdbath or sundial face. Is it worth adding a new top if I can't find one that matches its age?

A Yes, definitely. You'll sometimes find yourself with a pedestal that's crying out for a birdbath to be set on top of it, or with a sundial face that needs a base to sit on, and if you can't find what you're looking for in matching old stone, your only option may be to shop around local garden centres. The partnership of old and new may look out of place at first if the colours or textures jar, but give them time to find their own style and weather the elements together, and an odd couple will gradually marry successfully.

You shouldn't need to attach the two pieces together: an original birdbath would have simply been balanced on its pedestal by the stone mason. But if it wobbles or won't sit comfortably, you could grind the under surface of the bath to create a flatter base or, as a last resort, add a dab of mortar to fix it.

Q What's the best way to age new statuary and garden stonework to make it look more established?

A Even the most absorbent stone will take time to acquire a patina of age, but you can speed up the process by increasing its exposure to the corrosive effects of weather. Your best course is to check what experts say about undoing the damage caused to stonework by environmental conditions – and then do precisely the opposite. Conservators and restorers bring statuary indoors during winter to prevent the growth of lichen and algae; they keep it well away from sprinklers and damp overhanging foliage; and regularly remove ivy tendrils and other leaves that will collect water and create acid solutions. So to encourage lichen and algae, turn that advice on its head.

❍ Position your statue in a shady part of the garden, beneath a spreading tree or in woodland.

❍ Keep it damp: during warm weather. If it dries out, spray it with water to dampen the surface.

❍ Keep it out of direct sunshine. Sunlight – for all its ageing properties when you are dealing with paper, paintings, fabric and furniture – is remarkably harmless with regard to stonework.

❍ To speed things up if the statuary remains stubbornly new-looking, coat it with a layer of yogurt or liquid manure.

Q I've acquired a sort of latter-day Venus de Milo – a statue that was complete when I bought her but lost an arm during the journey home. Is there any way I can repair the damage?

A There are glues available for this type of repair, but unfortunately most of them won't survive many years in daylight, which is why most stone masons will use cement resin instead. If you think your statue is a good piece and really worth restoring, take it to a mason, who will mix up the right cement – probably by taking some of the original stone dust, then mixing it with cement and white adhesive so that it will match the piece and will age in sympathy with it.

But if she's not particularly valuable, your Venus is probably best left armless and interesting. There's a good precedent for it, after all, and if you position her carefully she'll create a sense of instant history in your garden. It shouldn't be too difficult to train greenery around her, or disguise her handicap amid a clump of tall cottage-garden lupins or foxgloves.

Don't attempt to mend garden statuary by pinning the breaks with metal dowels – they will gradually rust and expand, eventually causing even more cracks in the stone. A professional restorer would probably use conservation-grade stainless steel, but it's not really worth going to such lengths unless the piece is valuable, and then to seek professional advice.

Above: Stone statuary will age attractively when subjected to natural weathering: keep it cool and damp to encourage the growth of lichen.

glass

Glass has an almost miraculous quality that can make even the simplest pieces seem like domestic magic. The technique discovered more than 5,000 years ago enjoyed its heyday in 17th-century Venice but still exerts a fascination for designers today, with contemporary craft pieces providing a restrained contrast to the ornate decorations of the Victorian age. Extraordinarily versatile for something so fragile, glass is a fundamental part of our homes – in everything from windows to light bulbs – and yet has limitless decorative possibilities. Dining room tableware and hand-crafted perfume bottles demonstrate how well its practical and ornamental functions combine, and droplet-hung chandeliers perfect this art.

Sparkling and reflective, glass brings rooms instantly to life, responding to the light and providing interest and movement in gloomy corners. Clear or coloured, plain or engraved, clouded or iridescent – in all its variety, glass is irresistibly collectable, and often needs no more than thorough cleaning to revive its lustre. It's remarkably unpretentious, too, with gaudy carnival glass providing as much enjoyment as elegant decanters, and machine-engraved tumblers mixing comfortably with hand-cut crystal.

Q I've found an old mirror that has a very beautiful frame but badly damaged glass. Is there any point in repairing or replacing it?

A Mirrors used to be made by pouring silver nitrate from a jug over a sheet of glass, and adjusting the glass by hand until it was totally covered by an even layer of silver. Once dry, it would have been coated with varnish to protect both silver and glass from damp. Over time, this silvered backing would gradually chip off, creating dark, non-reflective patches on the surface, and might also be penetrated by damp, which fogs the glass.

Whether you do anything to repair your mirror depends really on whether it's more important to you as a practical looking glass or as a beautiful object. It will be fairly easy to have it professionally resilvered if you want, but this will be done by a modern technique: they will strip off the old silver with acid, brush tinning solution onto the back and spray on a new layer of silver nitrate. It will then be repainted to cover the silver, and sprayed with copper solution to protect against damp.

But there's a certain charm about the distressed glass of old mirrors, and it usually makes a much more natural match with an antique frame. At least half the beauty of an old looking glass is likely to be in its frame – whether gilded wood or decorative glass – and this is not diminished by a less-than-perfect mirror. You may find that a sparkling new sheet of glass looks totally wrong inside the older frame, and if the mirror has any value as an antique this will almost certainly be compromised by adding modern glass.

---

to clean mirror glass

A traditional method of removing marks is to rub the mirror with the cut surface of a raw potato, then polish with newspaper. To hide scratches, try mixing a little brass or silver polish with some toothpaste. Apply to the scratches with a lint-free cloth, leave for a few minutes, then polish to remove the excess.

Right: An attractive frame is half the beauty of an old mirror, so don't rush to replace damaged or 'foxed' glass.

Above: Lemon juice will help to remove marks from glassware: add a few ground eggshells to loosen limescale.

Q I've picked up an old decanter and set of matching sherry glasses. I liked the shape, so the fact that there are a few chips in the rims didn't deter me – but is it worth repairing them?

A You've bought them for the best possible reason – because you liked them – so think carefully before you risk further damage by attempting to repair them. If the decanter rim is badly chipped there won't be much you can do about it without getting professional help. A glass specialist will probably grind down the neck to remove the chip and keep the rest of the rim level. As an alternative in some cases a specialist may fit a silver collar around the neck to disguise the flaw. This is a good solution if you have a matching pair of decanters and so want to keep the necks the same length, but it's rather an elaborate treatment for a simple design.

However, if the chip is small, or you discover small nicks in the rim of a drinking glass, these are easier to tackle at home. Holding the item

carefully, rub gently at the uneven edge with a damp pumice stone, as though you were filing a snagged nail. It's important that the pumice is damp, because the water acts as a lubricant so that it polishes as it grinds – otherwise you'll end up with a frosted surface like one that's been scratched by constant washing in a dishwasher.

Q What's the best way of cleaning clouded or stained glass?

A Limescale and other deposits can gradually create a cloudy surface, which is particularly visible on clear glass. There are various ways of removing this. You could first try soaking the glass in a mixture of one part household ammonia to four parts warm water, or wiping it with a damp cloth and a paste mixed from 1 tablespoon each of vinegar and salt. If neither of these will shift the marks, or there are internal stains you can't reach, try one of the following remedies.

❍ For bottles and decanters where the narrow neck makes it more difficult to clean the inside, use a long-handled, medium-textured bottle brush. Brush with lemon juice, or a weak solution of proprietary scale remover or denture cleaner.

❍ For more awkward shapes (such as ship's decanters, which spread out at the bottom into a wide, shallow base into which a brush won't reach), pour in a little lemon juice mixed with ground-up eggshells, and shake thoroughly. The lemon will attack the limescale, and the grittiness of the shells will help work it loose from the glass.

If the marks still won't shift, you may have to send the item to a specialist to be acid-cleaned. Or it's possible that the cloudiness is due to very fine scratching or crazing caused by scouring or by washing in a dishwasher, in which case you won't be able to remove it. You could, however, distract attention from it by decorating the glass using one of the ideas for frosting or etching on pages 110–111.

GENERAL CARE OF GLASSWARE

❍ If a decanter stopper is stuck, smear olive oil around the join and leave it for about an hour to give it a chance to seep in. Then submerge the decanter in hot water – this will expand the body and you should be able to remove the stopper. Lift it out vertically, without twisting it.

❍ If you lose or break a stopper, keep a lookout for old ones in antiques shops and flea markets – they're often sold individually and you should be able to find one that fits.

❍ Don't leave any liquid standing in a decanter for too long: alcohol may stain and water may leave limescale.

❍ Always wash delicate glassware by hand – it won't stand up to the high temperatures of a dishwasher. Wash pieces one at a time, and if you're worried about knocking them, line the sink with a tea towel for protection.

to prevent lime build-up

Glass is particularly prone to build-up of limescale if it isn't dried properly after being washed. Damp left inside will gradually accumulate as lime, and will also promote condensation, so that the problem becomes a vicious circle. To dry the inside of a decanter or bottle if you can't get at it with a cloth, drop in a piece of rag or a couple of broad shoelaces, taping one end to the outside so that you can pull them out again. These will act as a wick and soak up any excess moisture. Keep turning the decanter so that the wick stays in contact with the moisture in the base until it is all absorbed.

Q I've amassed a huge collection of assorted tumblers and wine glasses. I've found uses for the best of them, but am left with a handful of plain ones that I'd like to decorate – any ideas?

A The following inspiring projects for engraving and frosting plain glass will transform anything from an old jam jar to a plain but elegant decanter that you'd like to personalize – perhaps with a name, a monogram or an important date.

Easy engraving

Engraving kits, available from craft shops and mail order suppliers, include engraving tools in different sizes – the point fits into a holder so that you can use it like a pen. This method of engraving needs to be done on an open container such as a goblet or vase, as a template is fixed to the inside of the glass.

1 Decide on the letter, name or date you want to engrave, trace the relevant characters from a book of typefaces and use a photocopier to scale it to the right size for your design.

2 Position the tracing on the inside of the glassware, carefully taping it in place with strips of masking tape.

3 Use the finest engraving tool to trace around the outline of the design on the outside of the glass. Now remove the template and replace it with a piece of black felt or paper pressed against the glass from the inside so that your outline is clearly visible.

4 Use a broader engraving tool to fill in the etched outline, working from the top of each character downwards and scratching the surface of the glass with a consistent pressure until it is evenly white.

Right: You can use a simple engraving kit to decorate plain second-hand glassware and create special effects or monogrammed details.

Instant etching

A proprietary spray-on etching can be used for the reverse effect, to create a frosted or sandblasted effect with the decoration left in clear glass. When using this product, wear a protective face mask and goggles and work in a well-ventilated room. Note that glassware decorated in this way cannot be immersed in water.

1 Cut your design out of paper and stick it onto the glass with spray adhesive. Or you can create a

banded or chequered pattern by applying strips or squares of masking tape.

2 Spray the entire surface with a light coat of the etching spray. Leave to dry for about 10 minutes, then add further coats, one at a time, depending on how opaque you want the effect to be.

3 When you are happy with the thickness of the frosting, wait until it is completely dry and then peel off the tape or paper templates to reveal the clear glass.

etched patterns

It's a good idea to build up a file of patterns and designs you like that could be used to decorate glassware and other surfaces.

Q I've found an old electric chandelier – very romantic and reminiscent of an old French château – but quite a few of the crystals are chipped or missing (which is presumably why it was cheap enough for me to afford it). Can I replace them?

A Electric chandeliers, with candle-shaped bulbs instead of real candles, date back to the beginning of the 20th century. The small, low-wattage bulbs shed a diffuse light that is soft and reflective, a little like real candlelight. This is effectively multiplied by the dangling crystals, with both rounded droplets and faceted pieces giving a prismatic, iridescent sparkle. The best examples of these chandeliers fetch very high prices and need professional cleaning and restoration, but there are many simpler designs – mostly from France and Italy – that, although very decorative, are less formal and therefore more suited to rustic settings. They look just as good in kitchens and bathrooms as in the more usual sitting room and bedroom settings.

It's also worth bearing in mind that the second-hand market will soon be boosted by a good number of modern reproductions that look fairly authentic once they've lost their newness. They may start life in department stores, but with a little distressed paintwork and a few natural dents they'll do a pretty good job of summoning up rural elegance.

Replacement crystals of various shapes and sizes are fairly easy to find, so it's surprising that the seller of your chandelier hadn't already replaced the missing ones in order to charge a higher price. Specialist companies will copy a missing part if you send them a sample, and boxes of mixed crystals can be found at auctions and antique markets. New crystals, very similar to old designs, are often imported from India and available in shops selling decorative accessories. These include an assortment of elongated peardrop shapes, long flat-surfaced shards and small glass globes, though mirrored droplets are more expensive and difficult to find.

FIXING AND CLEANING CHANDELIERS

Before you hang a chandelier, make sure the ceiling fitting will be strong enough to take the weight. You will need to screw this into a joist or have a metal plate fitted. If possible, attach it so that the chandelier can be unhooked and lowered when you need to clean it.

The droplets will have to be dismantled one by one, and can then be washed by hand in a detergent solution (take care not to let them chip one another). If you're concerned about reassembling them in the right order, you could take a photo for reference before dismantling, but don't worry too much if they don't go back in exactly the same way – the most important thing is that you're happy with the effect.

Left: A decorative chandelier will add romance and drama to traditional settings, especially if positioned where the light from the crystal droplets is multiplied by a mirror. Try adding extra droplets to match the colours in the room.

Q I can never resist buying old jewellery – nothing valuable, and often with unreliable stringing, but providing a wonderful array of beads and baubles. I'm never going to wear them, but I'd like to be able to make use of them somehow.

A There are whole shops and catalogues dedicated to beads these days, so you're in good company. They have become the quickest, easiest way to add decoration to furnishing accessories – adding jewel-like glamour to plain surfaces and transforming everything from curtains to lampshades. Some will be easy to unthread, providing handy holes for reusing; others will need to be prised from their settings but will then be perfect for sticking onto flat surfaces. Smaller beads can be stitched into tapestry or needlepoint like old-fashioned beadwork, or threaded into fringes to trim cushions or Art Deco-style lampshades.

Light pulls

Replace the standard plastic toggle or wooden acorn on the end of the pull-cord with a few heavy beads. Thread them onto the cord and secure with a knot or tassel.

Tablecloths and jug or tray covers

Stitch them around the edges of tablecloths to anchor the cloth with little decorative weights. Trim squares of muslin with beads to make old-fashioned jug and tray covers.

Napkin and candle rings

Thread beads onto circles of elastic or coils of fuse wire to create pretty napkin rings. Use the same technique to create candle rings in different sizes, slotting them over the candle to provide a decorative trim around the holder or base.

Cushions and curtains

Give plain furnishings a decorative finish. Stitch a sprinkling of beads onto sheer muslin for romantic bedroom curtains, or onto organza cushions to highlight the shimmering fabric.

Frames and boxes

Stud small trinket boxes and the frames of mirrors and pictures with bead patterns for a rich, jewelled effect.

Hanging droplets

Stitch beads around the lower edge of a lampshade or a curtain pelmet (cornice), or thread them onto wires so that they can be hooked into position like Christmas tree decorations. Hook them onto candle holders or use them to add extra colour amid the crystals of a chandelier.

Q My local flea market sometimes sells coloured glass magic-lantern slides. How can I make use of them?

A Magic lanterns created early film shows, providing the Victorians with colourful entertainment when they were tired of party games and singing around the piano. The lantern, an electric light projector, cast the pictures onto a screen in sequence to tell a story – frequently a Bible story or traditional morality tale. The earliest slides were hand-painted, while later versions (up to the 1930s) were printed. The slides are fairly easy to come by. Some have solid wooden frames; others are edged with adhesive paper tape or a brass frame. The trouble is that the original lanterns themselves are rarely found today. You can't use a normal projector instead because it isn't the right size (and wouldn't magnify the image enough anyway) and the only modern alternatives – such as the devices used to project high-tech clockfaces onto office walls – are very expensive. But the slides themselves are so charming and beautifully illustrated that it's a shame not to make use of them.

The best solution is to think of them as stained-glass panels and use them to make transparent pictures. Any position where the light will shine through them will be effective, so prop them in front of a lamp on a side table, display them in a back-lit china cabinet or, best of all, set them in a

window. In small windows they could be fitted into the windows as panels. Each slide makes a complete picture, but if you come across a boxed set telling a whole story, such as a fairy-tale, this would make a wonderful decoration for the window in a child's bedroom.

Above: A row of glass droplets stitched along a lace window trim catches the light for extra effect.

If the slides need cleaning, wipe the reverse side with a damp cloth and a little detergent, but take care not to get moisture on the image itself.

Q I've bought a set of tea plates, some of which have a fine tracery of cracks over the surface and blotchy marks on the pattern. What is the cause and is there any remedy?

A The glaze on china can crack or 'craze' if it's poorly looked after or subjected to extreme heat – if you look at the bottom of a teapot you will sometimes see fine crazing marks caused by the repeated contact with boiling water. Once the glaze is damaged it is no longer waterproof, which means that oil, grease and juices from food can seep underneath, staining the clay base of the china and highlighting the cracks themselves so that they show up as a filigree of dark lines. The staining will be worse in pottery than porcelain, because pottery is softer and more absorbent; porcelain is made from a fine white clay base that is almost impermeable.

There's no way of resealing the glaze, so you may find that the crazed plates continue to acquire stains if you use them regularly. But it's a shame to banish them to the display cabinet if they are otherwise sound. First, soaking the plates overnight in bleach may reduce the staining. Then, to tackle any dark lines along the cracks, soak a piece of cotton wool (absorbent cotton) in peroxide, and dab at the cracks. For stubborn marks, leave it on the cracks overnight. Don't use bleach or peroxide on plates decorated with lustre gilding, however, as these embellishments won't stand up to such aggressive cleaning.

Q I have occasionally come across floral chintz china of different ages. What period should I look for, and how do I care for it?

A The huge popularity of chintzware is easy to understand: its very pretty transfer patterns and colours, designed in imitation of printed cotton fabrics, are charming rather than elegant, making the china perfect for everyday use as well as display. It first appeared in the early 19th century, as inexpensive earthenware ranging from tea sets and flower vases to bedroom pitchers and washbasins. By the end of the century, a growing number of potteries were producing their own chintz designs, but it wasn't until the 1920s, with the mass production of Royal Winton, that the style blossomed into the familiar cottagey, densely sprigged patterns associated with chintzware. This is the most popular period for collectors, who enjoy the unusual combination of the traditional patterning with the slightly brighter colours and the distinctive angular shapes of the Art Deco era. Royal Winton, Crown Ducal, James Kent and Shelley are all names to look out for.

For once, in a rare example of topsy-turvy collectability value, the earlier pieces are cheaper to find, so you may be able to pick up Victorian chintzware bargains. These were printed in one colour, with contrasting details added by hand. The patterns tend to be looser and less dense than those of later chintzware and often incorporate Chinese-style motifs such as butterflies and birds. They may not be so typical of the genre, but they are interesting as examples of the transfer process. The unglazed earthenware was coated with a layer of size and a sheet of the lithographed design was pressed onto it. The backing was then removed, transferring the pattern to the china, which was finally glazed to make it waterproof.

Chintzware is still being made today, so faithful reproductions of traditional designs are available brand new. These are unlikely to turn up second-hand (as they will probably have been bought by collectors who have scoured flea markets and antiques shops for pieces) but you could consider adding a few new pieces to an older set. It will be just as appealing to collectors of the future.

Chintzware was made to be used, so it doesn't need kid-glove treatment. Use it as the Victorians did – for serving teas or pretty puddings, and wash it normally (but avoid dishwashers as these may remove the pattern and any gilding).

Right: Traditional floral chintzware makes a beautiful display on a dresser and is the perfect china on which to serve afternoon tea.

Above: A row of glass droplets stitched along a lace window trim catches the light for extra effect.

window. In small windows they could be fitted into the windows as panels. Each slide makes a complete picture, but if you come across a boxed set telling a whole story, such as a fairy-tale, this would make a wonderful decoration for the window in a child's bedroom.

If the slides need cleaning, wipe the reverse side with a damp cloth and a little detergent, but take care not to get moisture on the image itself.

Q There's always a good supply of old bottles of different types and colours at my local flea market. Can I make practical use of them rather than just keeping them for decorative display?

A As long as you can clean the interiors thoroughly, there's no reason why you shouldn't use them for cooking accessories such as oils and vinegars, or for scented oils in the bathroom. The smaller shapes can be transformed into decorative perfume bottles for a dressing table. Even beer bottles can be put to use, especially the type with sprung, air-tight lids, which are perfect containers to go in kitchen pantries. Lidless bottles can be fitted with corks or glass stoppers: keep a lookout for old stoppers from cruets and decanters, which are often sold separately in flea markets and antiques shops.

You'll give your bottles a far more professional finish (and turn them into very presentable gifts, too) if you trim them with attractive labels and other decoration. Decant store-bought or homemade oils and vinegars into elegant flasks and tall bottles, then string old-fashioned luggage labels around the necks to identify the flavour. Decorate each scent bottle with ribbon or cord tied in a loose bow, or wind silk thread tightly around the neck to cover it completely, ending with a tassel or a beaded knot. Paste a Victorian-style hearts-and-flowers label on the front and fill the bottle with a traditional perfume such as rosewater or lavender.

Below: Second-hand scent bottles can be trimmed with silk cord or homemade labels to create pretty dressing table and bathroom accessories.

Q Can I install old panels of etched glass or leaded lights from a salvage centre?

A Acid-etching was developed around the turn of the 18th century to create frosted, obscured-glass effects. This was originally for decoration, but the practical benefits made it popular, too. You may also come across sandblasted glass: the technique was patented at the end of the 19th century to do the same thing more cheaply, and it's not easy to tell the difference. Some glass will have an overall repeat pattern, like fabric or wallpaper, but you may also find panels designed as individual sections complete with a border – or perhaps etched with a house name or number, or lettering from a pub window. Etched glass can be fitted as normal into a door or window frame (keep the patterned side facing inwards, as the etched surface will attract dirt), or you can use a smaller section behind a bathroom washbasin. Ask a glass merchant to drill holes through the corners so that you can screw it into place, and position it with the etched side against the wall to protect the textured pattern.

Leaded lights – the patterned windows created from small panes of plain or coloured glass held together by lead 'cames' – can sometimes be salvaged from 19th- and early 20th-century houses, where they were standard decoration. Check the condition of the lead, as this can become weakened by atmospheric pollution. If it is brittle or cracked, or sections of glass are working loose, the panel will need professional releading. Think about the size of the window, too. It's unlikely that your panel will fit exactly, and reducing or enlarging leaded lights isn't an easy job. What you could do, however – particularly if the lead is already weakened – is either preserve the best parts of the window and create a new border around it, or ditch the overall design and find new uses for the glass. Look out for windows containing roundels (circular glass sections) and jewels (small, faceted pieces set among flat panes to catch the light), which can be wired or drilled through to use as chandelier crystals or hanging decorations.

CLEANING ETCHED GLASS

Use a soft brush dipped in undiluted household bleach, rubbing it into the textured surface with small circular strokes. Repeat the process after 30 minutes, then wash the glass thoroughly with soapy water.

CLEANING LEADED LIGHTS

Brush the lead with a small brush dipped in moistened scouring powder, then wipe it with a rag. Wash the glass with warm, soapy water, paying particular attention to the edges of each piece as more dirt can collect along the lead fixings. To darken the lead, you can use grate polish applied with a shoe brush, working along the line of the came; if you get any on the glass, this can be wiped off with white spirit (mineral spirits) on a rag.

glass marbles

Traditional glass marbles have been in regular production since the 19th century, and their rainbow colours make them wonderful decorations. Antique marbles can fetch quite a price, but you may find modern versions in more plentiful supply.

❍ Display them in glass dishes along a windowsill where their twists of colour will catch the light.

❍ Put a layer of marbles in the base of glass vases as additional decoration when arranging flowers.

❍ Fill a couple of flat-sided glass tanks with marbles and use them as bookends – the marbles will help to weight the containers to make them more stable.

❍ Wrap individual marbles in twists of wire mesh to create coloured droplets that can be hung from chandeliers or used to trim other accessories.

ceramics

Q I've bought a set of tea plates, some of which have a fine tracery of cracks over the surface and blotchy marks on the pattern. What is the cause and is there any remedy?

A The glaze on china can crack or 'craze' if it's poorly looked after or subjected to extreme heat – if you look at the bottom of a teapot you will sometimes see fine crazing marks caused by the repeated contact with boiling water. Once the glaze is damaged it is no longer waterproof, which means that oil, grease and juices from food can seep underneath, staining the clay base of the china and highlighting the cracks themselves so that they show up as a filigree of dark lines. The staining will be worse in pottery than porcelain, because pottery is softer and more absorbent; porcelain is made from a fine white clay base that is almost impermeable.

There's no way of resealing the glaze, so you may find that the crazed plates continue to acquire stains if you use them regularly. But it's a shame to banish them to the display cabinet if they are otherwise sound. First, soaking the plates overnight in bleach may reduce the staining. Then, to tackle any dark lines along the cracks, soak a piece of cotton wool (absorbent cotton) in peroxide, and dab at the cracks. For stubborn marks, leave it on the cracks overnight. Don't use bleach or peroxide on plates decorated with lustre gilding, however, as these embellishments won't stand up to such aggressive cleaning.

Q I have occasionally come across floral chintz china of different ages. What period should I look for, and how do I care for it?

A The huge popularity of chintzware is easy to understand: its very pretty transfer patterns and colours, designed in imitation of printed cotton fabrics, are charming rather than elegant, making the china perfect for everyday use as well as display. It first appeared in the early 19th century, as inexpensive earthenware ranging from tea sets and flower vases to bedroom pitchers and washbasins. By the end of the century, a growing number of potteries were producing their own chintz designs, but it wasn't until the 1920s, with the mass production of Royal Winton, that the style blossomed into the familiar cottagey, densely sprigged patterns associated with chintzware. This is the most popular period for collectors, who enjoy the unusual combination of the traditional patterning with the slightly brighter colours and the distinctive angular shapes of the Art Deco era. Royal Winton, Crown Ducal, James Kent and Shelley are all names to look out for.

For once, in a rare example of topsy-turvy collectability value, the earlier pieces are cheaper to find, so you may be able to pick up Victorian chintzware bargains. These were printed in one colour, with contrasting details added by hand. The patterns tend to be looser and less dense than those of later chintzware and often incorporate Chinese-style motifs such as butterflies and birds. They may not be so typical of the genre, but they are interesting as examples of the transfer process. The unglazed earthenware was coated with a layer of size and a sheet of the lithographed design was pressed onto it. The backing was then removed, transferring the pattern to the china, which was finally glazed to make it waterproof.

Chintzware is still being made today, so faithful reproductions of traditional designs are available brand new. These are unlikely to turn up second-hand (as they will probably have been bought by collectors who have scoured flea markets and antiques shops for pieces) but you could consider adding a few new pieces to an older set. It will be just as appealing to collectors of the future.

Chintzware was made to be used, so it doesn't need kid-glove treatment. Use it as the Victorians did – for serving teas or pretty puddings, and wash it normally (but avoid dishwashers as these may remove the pattern and any gilding).

Right: Traditional floral chintzware makes a beautiful display on a dresser and is the perfect china on which to serve afternoon tea.

ceramics

There's nothing quite so collectable as china. The small scale of individual pieces makes it temptingly easy to acquire and, once acquired, endlessly portable, however many times you move house. There's always room for one more piece – and always that sense of fragility to remind us that more might be needed, that we can lose old pieces as unexpectedly as we find new ones. The truth is that the price of getting full enjoyment from china, using it as well as displaying it, is the likelihood of having to sacrifice a few pieces along the way. The sleek lines and decorative surfaces that make it so attractive also make it vulnerable. There's enormous variety to be found – from chunky earthenware and ceramic tiles to delicately glazed porcelain, but although the homelier pieces may withstand slightly more robust treatment, ultimately their rigid brittleness makes them breakable too.

But its fragility is no reason to wrap your china in cotton wool. Even if it is no longer in good enough condition to be used, it's better displayed on a kitchen dresser or plate rack than hidden away behind closed doors. At any rate, favourite pieces are not necessarily those that are in perfect condition. What makes a piece attractive are shape and colour, which won't be spoiled by the odd chip or scratch. Even cracked pieces can look good, though they can't be used for liquids or subjected to heat.

Don't feel you need to look for complete sets: single items and 'orphans' from long-broken sets have their own charm and can be just as satisfying for collectors. In fact, a group of different patterns in the same colours often looks more interesting than a matching set. Don't worry about trying to track down old or valuable pieces either. Be cautious about spending a lot without checking the quality, but, beyond that, trust in what you like rather than what you think you ought to like. There's no better guide than your own taste.

Q I've found a tiled grate that's just the right size for my fireplace, but several of the tiles are chipped or missing. What's the best way of replacing them?

A Tiled grates can often be found more or less complete, and the best time to make any necessary repairs is before you fix the grate in place, as it is usually easier to remove the tiles at this point.

Replacing a missing tile

If a tile is missing completely, you have various options. Assuming that you want to recreate the original design, you can paint a new tile to match the missing one. Using a soft-lead pencil, take a tracing from one of the remaining tiles. Transfer it to a plain white or cream unglazed tile of the same size by placing the pencil side of the tracing face down on the tile and drawing over the traced lines with a hard-lead pencil. (The transferred image will be the reverse of the original, so, depending on the design, you may need to redraw the traced lines on the other side of the tracing paper, using a soft-lead pencil, before transferring it to the tile.) Now paint in the colours with ceramic paints, and glaze with clear polyurethane varnish.

Another option, if you don't trust your painting skills, is to commission a specialist tile shop to

paint you a new tile to order. They will be able to copy an existing one if you give them a sample to work from.

A more interesting approach, however, would be to mix a few odd tiles into the design, picking up the colours in a plain glaze or a contrasting pattern. Some colours and patterns mix particularly well: the traditional blue and white of delft-style tiles can easily be combined with contemporary tiles in those shades, in the same way that blue and white china mixes effortlessly on the shelves of a dresser.

Whichever approach you opt for, the tile will need to be sanded down on both side edges. Holding the tile with some tape stuck to the front of the tile, apply plaster of Paris to the side grooves of the grate and the back of the tile. Slot the tile into one groove and then slide it into the other. Clean any excess plaster from the surface, and hold the tile in place till the plaster sets.

Above: Tiled fireplaces are often found second-hand. Damaged tiles can be restored or replaced to complete the original pattern.

Repairing a broken tile

Because the tiles are held in place by the cast-iron framework of the grate, there's no urgent need to replace or repair a tile that's merely cracked, as the pieces are unlikely to shift. But if compound cracks have caused the decorative surface to chip, or part of the tile to loosen and fall out, you can repair the gaps rather than replacing the whole thing. Simply fill them with grout to provide a plain background level with the rest of the tile, then use ceramic paint to complete the missing part of the design. When dry, glaze with polyurethane varnish.

Q I've bought a set of tea plates, some of which have a fine tracery of cracks over the surface and blotchy marks on the pattern. What is the cause and is there any remedy?

A The glaze on china can crack or 'craze' if it's poorly looked after or subjected to extreme heat – if you look at the bottom of a teapot you will sometimes see fine crazing marks caused by the repeated contact with boiling water. Once the glaze is damaged it is no longer waterproof, which means that oil, grease and juices from food can seep underneath, staining the clay base of the china and highlighting the cracks themselves so that they show up as a filigree of dark lines. The staining will be worse in pottery than porcelain, because pottery is softer and more absorbent; porcelain is made from a fine white clay base that is almost impermeable.

There's no way of resealing the glaze, so you may find that the crazed plates continue to acquire stains if you use them regularly. But it's a shame to banish them to the display cabinet if they are otherwise sound. First, soaking the plates overnight in bleach may reduce the staining. Then, to tackle any dark lines along the cracks, soak a piece of cotton wool (absorbent cotton) in peroxide, and dab at the cracks. For stubborn marks, leave it on the cracks overnight. Don't use bleach or peroxide on plates decorated with lustre gilding, however, as these embellishments won't stand up to such aggressive cleaning.

Q I have occasionally come across floral chintz china of different ages. What period should I look for, and how do I care for it?

A The huge popularity of chintzware is easy to understand: its very pretty transfer patterns and colours, designed in imitation of printed cotton fabrics, are charming rather than elegant, making the china perfect for everyday use as well as display. It first appeared in the early 19th century, as inexpensive earthenware ranging from tea sets and flower vases to bedroom pitchers and washbasins. By the end of the century, a growing number of potteries were producing their own chintz designs, but it wasn't until the 1920s, with the mass production of Royal Winton, that the style blossomed into the familiar cottagey, densely sprigged patterns associated with chintzware. This is the most popular period for collectors, who enjoy the unusual combination of the traditional patterning with the slightly brighter colours and the distinctive angular shapes of the Art Deco era. Royal Winton, Crown Ducal, James Kent and Shelley are all names to look out for.

For once, in a rare example of topsy-turvy collectability value, the earlier pieces are cheaper to find, so you may be able to pick up Victorian chintzware bargains. These were printed in one colour, with contrasting details added by hand. The patterns tend to be looser and less dense than those of later chintzware and often incorporate Chinese-style motifs such as butterflies and birds. They may not be so typical of the genre, but they are interesting as examples of the transfer process. The unglazed earthenware was coated with a layer of size and a sheet of the lithographed design was pressed onto it. The backing was then removed, transferring the pattern to the china, which was finally glazed to make it waterproof.

Chintzware is still being made today, so faithful reproductions of traditional designs are available brand new. These are unlikely to turn up second-hand (as they will probably have been bought by collectors who have scoured flea markets and antiques shops for pieces) but you could consider adding a few new pieces to an older set. It will be just as appealing to collectors of the future.

Chintzware was made to be used, so it doesn't need kid-glove treatment. Use it as the Victorians did – for serving teas or pretty puddings, and wash it normally (but avoid dishwashers as these may remove the pattern and any gilding).

Right: Traditional floral chintzware makes a beautiful display on a dresser and is the perfect china on which to serve afternoon tea.

Q I'm on the lookout for original spongeware – how can I tell the age of any pieces I find?

Above: Printed spongeware patterns give china a naive, informal character perfect for country kitchens.

A The tradition of sponge-printed pottery can be traced back to 18th-century Staffordshire, when the designs were cut into pieces of sponge and then applied to plain china using a variety of cheerful pigment colours. (If the patterns look a little like a child's potato prints, it's not surprising: potato stamps, along with brushes and cloths, were sometimes used, too.) But from the 1820s onwards this pottery became popular across Europe – in France, Germany, the Netherlands and Portugal – and also in the United States, which eventually became the major focus of spongeware production from the end of the 19th century right through to the 1930s.

You're incredibly lucky if you find an original piece in a British market – simply because it was nearly all exported. What was left behind was treated very casually and subjected to tough everyday use – almost as disposable tableware that could be thrown away when chipped or cracked – so supplies gradually ran out. The few remaining pieces get snapped up by collectors for top prices. Rare pieces printed in a single colour (especially in black or yellow) are particularly collectable, as are designs with animal motifs – the more unusual the better. Don't expect to find any real bargains: the only way to pick up cheaper pieces is to look for items that are slightly cracked, or that include freehand brushstrokes among the printed patterns.

What you're more likely to come across are modern designs, still made today by names such as Brixton Pottery and Emma Bridgewater. These continue the simple, naive traditions of the original concept and have a timeless, comfortable style that is particularly suited to country kitchens, but they are quite easy to distinguish from the antiques. Modern spongeware – collectable purely for enjoyment rather than for rarity value – is always marked with the maker's name, unlike most older pieces, and the surface has a much smoother, more even texture.

How to display spongeware

The distinctive quality of spongeware patterning, with its soft edges and hand-blocked effects, creates a unifying style that allows contrasting designs and colours to work well together. Old and new spongeware designs will mix comfortably on a dresser or mantelpiece, and also blend successfully with other rustic-style pottery.

Q I've bought a box of old china very cheaply, for the sake of a few cups I really wanted. I'm now left with a lot of chipped oddments – how can I use the pieces?

A If you can bear to break up the remaining pieces, they would make wonderful ingredients for a homemade mosaic. It doesn't matter whether they are matching items; once you've reduced them to mosaic-size chips, you'll have plenty of each different pattern – enough to use individually or in combination, depending on the effect you want to create. Adding a mosaic surface is a satisfying way of decorating anything from trays and table tops to flowerpots and other containers. Because of its Mediterranean origins, mosaic is usually associated with bright chips of plain colour, but pastel shades and decorative patterned china can work just as well, giving a softer, prettier feel. You can employ the same technique to use up old ceramic tiles or their offcuts – the only difference is that they will be harder to break.

TO CREATE A MOSAIC SURFACE

1 Cover the china with a cloth (an old sheet or tea towel) and break it up with a hammer. Keep checking the size of the chips you're creating – you don't want to pound it into powder, but some items will be tougher than others. If you're using tiles, you'll need tile snippers to cut through them: aim for small pieces around 2.5cm (1in) square.

2 Select an item to decorate, clean the surface thoroughly and plan your mosaic design, working out how many pieces it will need. At this stage you can choose between a random mix of different colours and a more structured layout creating a definite picture or pattern. Or you can keep to a single type of ceramic to cover a smaller item such as a jug or flowerpot. For a flat surface such as a table top, it's a good idea to cut out a card template of the shape so that you can plan a complete design before transferring it into position.

3 Use a spreader to apply ceramic adhesive to the surface a little at a time, transferring your mosaic design as you go, by pressing the ceramic chips into the adhesive. With a curved item such as a vase, rest it between a couple of wooden blocks, or bricks padded with cloth, so that you can work on the exposed surface a section at a time; wait until the adhesive dries before turning it to work on the next section.

4 Once the pattern is fixed and the adhesive dry, work grout between the pieces. Wipe off the excess with a damp cloth and leave to dry (this may take a couple of days), then polish and buff the mosaic with a dust cloth.

Q What is the best way to display a set of plates that is probably too fragile for any practical use?

A Plates – even in the simplest of colours and designs – are tailor-made for display, and dressers and plate racks have for years been designed with this purpose in mind. The neatest of these have ridges or grooves in the shelves, to hold the plates in place and prevent them from slipping, as well as slats across the front. In most racks, your plate size will be limited by the shelf height, but if you're lucky you might come across a rack with slim ledges rather than full-width shelves. With these, the plates are simply slotted in and can lean forward against the front bars, allowing you to display larger sizes. Be careful how you line the plates up: don't prop them against one other or let them knock together.

Another option – which will also provide practical storage for plates that are still in regular use – is a traditional wooden draining rack with individual slots for each plate. Mounted over the sink or standing on a worktop, this is far better than stacking plates in a cupboard, where you risk chipping and scratching their surfaces. However, the fronts of the plates are not so visible, as the plates are stored at right angles to the wall.

To hang plates directly on the wall, you can use either plastic-covered wire holders or specially designed adhesive discs. A wire holder is quick and easy to fix in place over the back of a plate, but the grippers will be visible around the edges. For an invisible fixing, an adhesive disc, which incorporates a hook for hanging, is stuck to the back of the plate. The larger the disc, the heavier the plate it can safely hold (see the label for the manufacturer's recommendations). Moisten the adhesive side, leaving it for the specified time,

then press the disc into place, smoothing out any air bubbles. Now leave it long enough to achieve a secure fix before hanging. If you decide at a later date to take off the disc, it can be removed without trace simply by soaking in water.

Q Is there any point in buying old decorative tiles? I sometimes come across them but I don't know if they're sound enough to be put to practical use.

A Old tiles should be just as useful as modern ceramic tiles – with the same risks attached to cutting them (in other words, they can chip or crack if you're out of practice with the snippers). And, like modern tiles, they need to be laid on a completely flat surface. Check the batch you're buying to make sure that it's not harbouring any old adhesive or grouting, which will need to be ground or filed off before you can use them. You should then be able to install the tiles in a fireplace, or on a kitchen or bathroom wall. The only difference is that it's a good idea to use reversible grout so that, if you want to, you can remove the tiles again without damaging them. Think of them as decorative extras, though, and you'll be able to see more potential for them, because you don't need huge numbers to be able to use them to effect. Half a dozen tiles will create a decorative panel amid a run of plain tiles, or can be used on their own behind a washbasin, and a few more will provide a border around the room at chair rail height.

But the real pleasure of old tiles, and the reason that collectors become hooked once they get started, is that each individual tile creates a miniature picture in its own right – whether it is an abstract design from the Art Nouveau period or a complete figurative scene typical of blue and white Dutch delftware. Even tiles designed to be used as sets, where each one contributes just part of the image created by the whole panel, will generally have their own interest if used individually. Particular favourites can be framed for display – either singly, or perhaps as a panel of

<hr>

hanging plates

Don't hang cracked or mended plates – always use a shelf support of some kind.

Above: A random selection of second-hand tile designs can be worked into a wall of plain white in a kitchen or bathroom.

four – or simply displayed on a mantelpiece or shelf. You might use a few of them to give a small table a ceramic top, or line the underside with felt and use them as table mats or teapot stands. (Be aware, though, that the surface design is susceptible to scratching if you treat it harshly.)

delft tiles

New tiles made as reproductions of original delft designs are very authentic-looking – but feel the surface, both front and back. Newer tiles are much smoother, whereas the originals will have slight dips and dimples, and sometimes bubbles in the glaze.

127

Q How can I tell the age and quality of the china I buy? What clues should I look for to check its authenticity?

A Learning to spot the bargains and avoid the fakes is a lifelong process. Buy a good antiques guide to teach you the basics, and then trust your instincts. There's no rigid guide as to whether a newer piece in perfect condition is a better buy than something older but damaged: this will vary according to the type of china and how collectable it is. Your best bet is to buy it if you like it (and if the price is reasonable) and then ask an expert to supply the missing history.

Below: Pretty china abounds at flea markets, but you need to know what you're paying for.

How old is it?

First weigh the china in your hand. In general, the lighter it is for its size, the older it's likely to be. Then check the base for identifying marks. China made from the beginning of the 20th century onwards will be marked with its country of origin. If it's earlier than that, it may have a combination of numbers and squiggles (often pretty hard to decipher) – or in some cases no marks at all. Much Western china during the 1800s was made unmarked, partly because retailers didn't want to reveal their sources. Competition was so intense during this period that keeping ahead of other companies was considered more important than brand promotion. The trouble is that the absence of an identifying mark doesn't guarantee a pre-1900 date, because modern copies made in the Far East can be very convincing – so be careful.

is it pottery or porcelain?

Pottery, which includes earthenware and stoneware, is clay-based. Porcelain is made from a mixture of fine white china clay and china stone and can be fired to a higher temperature. Porcelain is always translucent (even if sometimes only slightly), so hold it up to the light to check whether you can see through it. Also look for unglazed areas on the base of any foot-rim (the projecting round base on the underside) – porcelain has a smooth, hard finish that is difficult to scratch even when unglazed.

Q How can I check whether a piece has been mended or restored in the past?

A It's always worth checking for signs of previous mending or restoration work before you buy, as a damaged piece, however well (and however discreetly) mended, won't stand up to normal use. It won't hold liquids effectively, may not stand up to heat, and probably can't be washed without weakening the mend. Also look for fine cracks that might have gone unnoticed so far but will eventually give way if you start using the item.

❍ The most obvious places to check are protrusions such as knobs, spouts and handles. Hold the piece carefully as you look, supporting the main body rather than letting the handle take the weight. (Also consider the proportions of the design: is the handle big enough to hold the weight of the item plus its contents? If not, it may have been designed purely for decoration in the first place.)

❍ Bear in mind that mends in the shadow of a joint may be difficult to spot – particularly if a water-soluble glue was used or the piece is too dirty to check properly (it could be worth taking a soft brush with you so that you can remove surface dirt). Look for discoloured paintwork – this may be recent decoration added to cover a mend. Iron rivets will be more obvious, as they are hard to disguise, but they will mean a stronger join, and are a sign of authenticity. They are part of the item's history so they shouldn't dissuade you from buying it if you particularly like it.

❍ If it's porcelain, check for warm patches. Porcelain should be cold to the touch and slightly gritty on the teeth, so warmer, smoother patches suggest restoration work. Run a pin over the surface: it will glide over the original glaze but catch on any softer restoration work. Also tap the edge carefully and listen to the sound: if it sounds flat rather than ringing clear, it has probably been mended at some point.

Signs of restoration shouldn't put you off buying china that you particularly like, but you'll have to be prepared to keep it for very light or purely decorative use if you want to prevent further damage. If it's part of a set, mark the restored pieces so that you don't use them by mistake. If you want to use a cracked or restored vase to display flowers, you can slip an additional container inside it to hold the water so that the outer vase remains dry.

TO MEND BROKEN CHINA

1 Swab the two pieces with acetone to remove any dust and greasy finger marks. Make sure they are completely dry, then carefully (without any grating) practise fitting them together so that you know what the correct join should feel like.

2 Using a two-tube epoxy resin, follow the manufacturer's instructions carefully. Apply a thin layer of adhesive (some restorers advise coating both edges, others only one, so follow the pack instructions), bring the edges carefully together so that the join feels properly aligned, then press the edges together.

3 You will need to keep the edges held in place while the bond sets, so stick a few 5–7.5cm (2–3in) lengths of cellophane tape across the mend and at right angles to it. You can also stand the item in a bowl of sand to give it a secure base and keep it steady while it sets.

4 Once it has set, remove any excess adhesive with a paintbrush dipped in methylated spirit (denatured alcohol), but be careful not to flood the join or you will weaken the new bond.

Q I couldn't resist buying a very pretty teapot, even though it was already cracked. Sure enough, the handle broke off almost immediately – is there any chance of mending it invisibly?

A The first thing to establish is whether the teapot is of any great age or value. This may be fairly obvious, or you may be able to work it out from running the checks suggested in the question about identifying pottery and porcelain on page 129, but if you're still in doubt, you'll need to consult a professional restorer. Collect up all the broken pieces (including the tiniest chips – these are all part of the jigsaw) but don't try to fit them together yourself, as the rough edges may

Right: Check very carefully for cracks and previous restoration work before you use china or immerse it in hot water. Be especially careful with handles, which may have become weakened.

grate and damage one another. Don't be tempted to tape the pieces onto paper, either, as the adhesive may damage the decoration. If you suspect the china may be valuable, the safest way to transport it is in a box, with each piece wrapped individually in acid-free tissue paper (see pages 148–156).

Assuming, however, that you (or the expert) have decided that it's nothing special, and that the break is fairly clean, there's nothing to stop you going ahead and mending it yourself (following the advice given on the left). Then, once it's mended, treat it carefully: don't pick it up by the handle, don't put hot liquids in it or submerge it in very hot water, and try to keep it for display only.

GENERAL CARE AND CLEANING

Ceramics aren't at risk from atmospheric conditions, but the biggest threats to them are clumsy handling and incorrect cleaning. To keep your china in good condition, follow these guidelines.

❍ Always remove lids before moving items such as teapots and tureens, and don't lift pieces by their handles or arms – they may not provide enough support and you also run the risk of weakening any past mends.

❍ If you have more items in a set than you need, use them in strict rotation so that wear – and risk – are spread equally.

❍ Don't put boiling water directly into fine china or porcelain. To warm plates and tureens, never put them in the oven, but immerse them in hot water for a couple of minutes.

❍ After use, remove any oily or greasy deposits quickly to prevent the china from absorbing them and being stained. When cleaning precious pieces, wash one piece at a time, and always rinse off detergent thoroughly. Don't put anything fragile or valuable – or any china decorated with lustre or gilding – into the dishwasher. Clean delicate items by dusting with a soft brush and wiping with a damp cloth or cotton wool (absorbent cotton) rather than submerging them in water.

Q I want to lay a traditional tiled floor in my kitchen. What is the difference between quarry and terracotta tiles – or are they the same thing?

A The two terms have become almost interchangeable, and the general effect is very similar: both are more or less terracotta-coloured and have a simple, practical look that is a natural choice for country kitchens. But in general, terracotta is used to describe pure clay tiles made by traditional methods, whereas quarries have come to mean the slightly smaller, smoother machine-made tiles more familiar in British homes built in the late 19th and early 20th centuries. Good-quality reclaimed tiles are in demand, so you may not get the luxury of choice, but it's worth knowing the difference and how to treat them.

The pure clay of terracotta (literally 'baked earth') provides a more rustic finish and more variety of colour – from pale pink and honey shades through the traditional orangey brown to deep burgundy. They are slightly porous, so will probably need sealing with linseed oil or a proprietary sealant to prevent the surface from becoming stained by water and grease.

Quarry tiles, on the other hand, include a high quartz content with their clay, and are fired at a higher temperature, making them less porous and very hard-wearing. Although unglazed, they are frost-proof and don't need sealing. (In fact, it's not a good idea to try, as the sealant may not be absorbed properly and may create a slippery surface.)

Old quarry and terracotta tiles varied in size and thickness, so if you are buying reclaimed tiles make sure that your batch came from the same original floor and can be laid evenly together. Variation in colour doesn't matter, as it simply adds more character, but different sizes will cause big problems.

Right: Old terracotta pots are worth looking out for as they have a mellow, weathered finish.

Q I love the traditional look of terracotta flowerpots: how can I tell the difference between old and new?

A The classic terracotta pot shape that we all recognize today dates back to Victorian gardens. Hand-thrown from quality clay, the original pots were frost-proof but also porous, so that they weathered beautifully and prevented the internal atmosphere from becoming stagnant and waterlogged. As well as the full pot size, they were available as shorter half pots, shallow seedpans and the distinctive longtoms, which were specially

designed to hold long-rooted plants. The appeal of longtoms is aesthetic rather than practical. Their tall, slim shape meant they were difficult to make and easy to knock over, so they were more often found indoors than outside where the wind might buffet them. The Victorians used them to grow lilies in greenhouses. You need to keep them in a sheltered place, or bed them into gravel to secure the bases.

Some specialist potteries still make the traditional designs today, individually thrown and using the old techniques. You probably won't be able to tell the difference between these and the originals they reproduce – but that doesn't really matter because they will still create an authentic effect in the garden and weather in the same way. It's more important that you are able to spot machine-made pots: there's no guarantee that these are frost-proof and you may spot cracks running down from the rims. These pots also tend to be externally glazed, which means they're not porous. Before you make a purchase, check the surface and look at the shape of the rims: machine-made pots have a much smoother surface than the hand-thrown designs, and the rims are broader and flatter.

other treasures

Flea markets and second-hand shops are full of unexpected finds to tempt the curious mind, many of them hard to classify under traditional collectors' categories. To make the most of them, open your imagination to all the practical and decorative possibilities they present. Some of them, like plastic, may be trying to simulate other materials; others – such as feathers and shells – will declare themselves quite openly as oddities, leaving you to contrive inventive uses for them. There's no common theme to make these finds a subject in which you can specialise. They range from intricately crafted pieces to far more functional, everyday items. It's up to you to identify what appeals to you and be prepared to adapt to their demands. Bear in mind that superficially similar materials such as wicker, cane and Lloyd Loom will actually require quite different care and cleaning techniques. And objects incorporating mixed media can't be treated as though they were made of the individual materials alone: old gardening tools will have both wood and metal parts for you to look after, while decorative fans may include elements as varied as fabric, paper, paintwork, embroidery, glass beads and metal sequins. The important thing is to train your eye to spot potential where it exists, and then have fun putting it to use.

Q What is Lloyd Loom furniture made of, and how should I look after it?

A The golden age of Lloyd Loom in Britain was the middle of the 20th century. Although it's still made today, it has a practical utility look about it that was somehow particularly suited to the war years. Strong and durable, it looks like hand-crafted wicker but is actually woven and plaited from paper reinforced with strands of steel wire. You can use a strong magnet to check that it's the real thing. You won't be able to spot joins in the weave because the paper fibre comes in much longer lengths than cane or rattan.

Invented in America in 1922 by Marshall Burns Lloyd, the furniture quickly became popular, with original designs including cakestands, lamps, firescreens and vases as well as the familiar chairs and tables. Production was mostly in the United States, but overseas licensees included Lusty of London, who had more than 400 Lloyd Loom designs in their 1933 catalogue. Lusty's went into liquidation at the end of the 1960s, but the furniture is still being made – in Britain by Lloyd Loom of Spalding and in the United States by Lloyd/Flanders, based in Marshall Burns Lloyd's original factory in Menominee, Michigan.

If you're buying second-hand Lloyd Loom, check the hardwood dowels of the framework for woodworm: look for the telltale boreholes and powder (see page 32), and make sure the structure doesn't feel rickety. Don't buy furniture that's badly damaged by worm, because it can't really be repaired. Also avoid pieces where the fibre has acquired a 'furry' look or a washed-out grey colour, and check for hairline cracks in the dowels. These symptoms suggest that the furniture has been dipped in a stripping tank or spent far too long in the garden, and there won't be much you can do to repair the damage.

Left: To check whether a chair is wicker or Lloyd Loom, use a magnet: Lloyd Loom uprights are reinforced with steel wire.

LLOYD LOOM REPAIRS

If any filler strands (the horizontal pieces that weave in and out of the wire-reinforced uprights) have snapped or frayed, they can be repaired with PVA woodworking glue, which creates a strong, transparent mend. Dab a tiny spot of glue on both the broken ends, then hold the join in place with masking tape while it dries. For larger holes in the weave, you can buy repair kits that include lengths of replacement fibre and the traditional braid edging from Lloyd Loom of Spalding, or take the item to a specialist restorer (see pages 148-156).

CLEANING

Remove dust from the weave with a hand-held vacuum cleaner, then test-wash a small area. If it still has the original paintwork, you should be able to scrub it lightly with a soft brush and soapy water, or hose it down in the garden. On a warm day it will dry in a couple of hours. If it's been repainted, you may need to use a damp cloth rather than a brush, to prevent the paint from flaking off.

REPAINTING

Pieces in the original colours, even if faded or worn, are more collectable, so repainting isn't necessarily a good idea and will almost certainly lower the resale value. If you decide to do it, start by cleaning the piece thoroughly to clear out the weave. Then use cellulose spray paint (from car body repair shops), spraying carefully and lightly so the weave doesn't get clogged up. You might prefer to ask the car shop to do it for you – or contact a specialist restorer (see pages 148-156).

Q I often see old gardening and workshop tools for sale in flea markets. Can they still be used as intended or are they now just curiosities?

A Like kitchen utensils, these old implements have a charm born of long use and personal significance. The trowels, hoes, shears and forks that have worked our gardens over the centuries were originally the property of the individual workers who used them; lathes and planes were often hand-made by their owners as part of a craftsman's apprenticeship. Heavy and worn, they feel totally different from their shiny, lightweight modern counterparts, but as long as they have been well looked-after – and as long as you continue to maintain them – they will be just as practical.

Simple tools designed for basic garden upkeep were hand-wrought (and mended) by blacksmiths until the Victorian era, when increasingly complex devices and mechanisms for specific tasks became popular and mass production took over. It's not always easy to gauge the exact age of a tool, because in some parts of the country blacksmiths went on making them by hand up to World War II, but you may be able to track down something of its past if it was mass-produced and has a brand name that appeared in a catalogue.

But, although serious collectors will want to fill in as much of its history as possible, for many people it will just be another practical garden tool, or another decorative object for the house. Heavy old implements – especially flat-bottomed things like planes – make excellent paperweights as well as intriguing shapes to display on a shelf or mantelpiece, and you won't have to worry too much about keeping them in perfect condition. If you want to use them practically, however, make sure that both wood and metal parts are in good shape. This is one area where restoration will have been in a good cause, and restored items are therefore likely to be more expensive.

TO KEEP TOOLS IN GOOD CONDITION

❍ Brush off loose soil after gardening, rinse in clean water and dry thoroughly.

❍ Oil the metal parts of spades, forks and hoes to help preserve them.

❍ Oil the moving parts of shears and secateurs (pruners) to keep the movement smooth.

❍ Sand wooden handles gently with fine paper or steel wool, then rub them with either linseed or teak oil.

❍ Keep knives, shears and secateurs (pruners) well sharpened.

❍ Store tools in a dry place.

Right: The smooth-worn wood of old garden tools feels comfortable to handle and adds a sense of history to the gardener's shed.

Q How old is 'old' plastic, and what problems should I check for?

A There's a long tradition of surfaces being decorated to look like something else, and the invention of plastic in the late 19th century opened up new possibilities for cheaper, more versatile imitations of more valuable materials.

Bakelite

This makes a positive virtue out of being synthetic. It's not pretending to be anything else,

Above: We may rely now on fax machines and email, but no old-fashioned study is complete without a classic black Bakelite telephone.

and although its original popularity had a lot do with being a good substitute for dark wood, it quickly became a style statement in its own right. Named after the Danish chemist Baekeland who invented it in 1907, it could be cut, moulded or drilled, and was the perfect material for the machine age – its heat-resistance made it practical

140

for things like ashtrays and hair dryers, and its mouldable quality allowed the manufacture of smooth, rounded Art Deco shapes. It was also used for colourful marbled picnicware and a lot of 1920s and '30s jewellery. Production of Bakelite stopped at the end of the 1930s as the world entered an era of function and utility, leaving us with an enduring image of classic black telephones and dark brown wartime 'wirelesses'.

Don't let nostalgia overrule your judgment: good Bakelite is usually only found at specialist dealers now and commands collectors' prices. Condition is important, because it can't be restored, so if you find it in a market, always check for discoloration and cracks or chips, and make sure electrical items and phones have been approved for use.

Simulated tortoiseshell

Tortoiseshell is still a classic finish for decorative hair combs and clips, but today's plastic accessories don't attempt to imitate the real thing as accurately as they once did. Genuine tortoiseshell (as well as having now become ecologically unacceptable) tended to fade and become brittle after prolonged exposure to light. It would sometimes crack, or develop patches of discoloration. As a more practical alternative, horn (usually stronger) was sometimes stained to look like tortoiseshell. Plastic, however, was even more versatile, and you're much more likely to come across this than the real thing. Simulated tortoiseshell was used for buttons, jewellery, hand mirrors and hair brushes, as well as decorative combs. It was made from an early form of celluloid, which incorporated camphor to make it less brittle, but in many cases the camphor has evaporated over the years, leaving the plastic more likely to snap, so be careful with delicate items such as combs.

Marbled fountain pens

Traditional pens with their swirly, slightly iridescent surfaces are small gems of elegant design, adding an instant touch of class to writing tables. But you want to be able to use them as well as enjoying their good looks, so check them carefully before you buy. Many are from the days before replaceable ink cartridges, so make sure the fixed rubber reservoir inside hasn't rotted – you probably won't be able to have it replaced. If it won't unscrew for you to check, ask if you can try filling it, to make sure the suction mechanism is working smoothly. Look for cracks, too, especially around the screw top of the nib section, which can be weakened by over-tightening. And make sure it doesn't leak – try it out on paper to check that the ink flow isn't too enthusiastic.

Q My local flea market sometimes sells game feathers – partridge, pheasant and so on. They're tempting to buy, but not particularly practical. How could I use them decoratively?

A Don't write off practical uses altogether – they make rather nice bookmarks, to start with. But they're really too pretty to keep hidden away between covers, so you need to find places to display them. Like shells and paintbrushes, they make effective pictures if you mount a row of them against a plain background and edge with a chunky wooden frame. If you think of how they were once used to trim clothes and dress accessories such as hats and cloaks, you'll find inspiration for decorating all sorts of home items, from lampshades to curtains. Far more simply, you can display a clutch of feathers in a vase on a window-sill or writing desk, so that they're reminiscent of quill pens, or weave them into an elegant wreath that can be hung on a wall or door. Wreaths aren't just for Christmas, and this glossy plumage can stay on show all year round.

To make a feather wreath

Twist a length of wire into a circle to make your base, then lash each feather onto it individually, by twisting fine wire or twine around the exposed spine end. Overlap the feathers quite thickly to conceal the fixings and to make the wreath look more luxurious, then hang on a hook or peg.

Q I love shell and pearl finishes, and have bought several bags of shells and mother-of-pearl buttons to use for decoration. How fragile are they?

A Handled with respect, shells – particularly the largest, chunkiest ones – are fairly robust and can be put to effective practical use. Scallops and oysters will make pretty soap dishes, or can be used to hold jewellery on a dressing table. Fill them with pearl bracelets or necklaces and they'll look like dishes of treasure scooped straight from the sea.

Smaller, thinner shells are more brittle and can chip or shatter if roughly treated, but are perfect for creating decorative trimmings. As long as they are fixed firmly in place so that they won't knock against one another, they should be safe from damage. Shells like these are often sold by weight in shops and markets. Environmentalists campaign against their removal from beaches, but the fact is, they are available and they do make beautiful decorations. Here are just a few of the many possibilities.

❍ Frame a selection of them in a deep box frame to hang on the wall.

❍ Glue them in a single line around the lower edge of a lampshade.

❍ Glue thick clusters of shells on a plain frame as a border for a mirror or photograph.

❍ Thread a few larger shells loosely onto cord or string to make curtain tie-backs.

❍ Line them up along a window-sill where their individual shapes – no two ever quite alike – will create intriguing silhouettes.

Mother-of-pearl, which if genuine is actually the inner surface of certain shells, is more delicate. It's created from dozens of very thin layers, which can flake or peel in dry conditions, so it's best kept out of direct sunlight and heat if possible. Take care when washing items trimmed with mother-of-pearl buttons as they are easily damaged. The other place you're likely to find it is as decorative inlay in woodwork. Try to avoid dusting or polishing these areas as fabric can snag on the inlay and cleaning products may collect around the edges.

Q I couldn't resist buying a bundle of artists' brushes – I don't paint, but they just looked so tempting. What on earth can I do with them?

A You don't need to be a fine artist to find practical uses for these neat-sized brushes.

Even if their tips are rather blunted and out of condition (which is probably the case if they've ended up on a market stall), they're still good enough for dusting intricate metalware, and for cleaning pictures and frames, as the brush will get into awkward corners that would be difficult for a cloth. Use them to dust the tops of books and the backs of clocks, where you don't want to jog the mechanism by rough handling. Clean up old mouldings and plasterwork, and retouch grimy corners without having to repaint the whole thing. Keep them handy for pasting and painting when you're working on decorative craft projects and quick home repairs.

But they do have a certain elegance, with their spindle-shaped wooden handles. A pot of mixed brushes on a desk or window-sill instantly conjures up something of the creative atmosphere of a studio. And a horizontal row of brushes framed in different lengths and shapes (flat-headed, round-tipped and so on) makes a distinctive picture for a study wall. Just remember, if you do use them, to clean and rinse them carefully and reshape the brush ends. Always store them brush-end up, so you don't crush or blunt the tips.

Below: Old brushes are useful for cleaning intricate and fragile possessions as well as coming in handy for the gluing and painting involved in craft projects.

Q There always seems to be masses of second-hand bone-handled cutlery for sale in flea markets. What's the best way to look after it?

A The important thing to remember with bone is that it is prone to crack if subjected to constant fluctuations in temperature and humidity. You need to check for signs of cracking before you buy, as well as taking care how you look after it. Look at the grain, too. Bone should have fine markings, slightly irregular in form, running through it. If you can't see any grain at all, it may be plastic masquerading as bone.

Don't attempt to wash bone-handled cutlery in a dishwasher. The heat and detergent will discolour the handles and may also loosen the glue, so that handle and implement are at risk of coming adrift. Instead, hand-wash in warm water (without immersing the handles or joins, as this, too, would weaken the adhesive) and dry immediately. Wiping the handles with vegetable oil will help to prevent the bone from drying and cracking, and an occasional polish with milk may revive the sheen if it has dulled.

Q I've found a beautiful old fan but I'm terrified that it will fall apart – what's the best way to look after it?

A The difficulty with fans is that each one incorporates so many different elements, some more robust than others. The frame, for instance, can be made of metal, or plastic, or an organic material such as ivory or tortoiseshell. The flexible part (known as the 'leaf'), on the other hand, may be made of paper, feather, kid, or any sort of fabric from lace to silk. And on top of that, it's likely to be decorated with embroidery, painting, stitched-on beads or other appliquéd trimmings. It therefore needs careful handling, and is rarely going to stand up to the sort of melodramatic treatment to which fans are traditionally subjected in television costume dramas. The only kind that can be snapped open or shut in a single flamboyant gesture is the Spanish fan, which is more robust – that's why it can be flourished and flicked so effectively as part of the flamenco dance routine.

If you want to use yours, perhaps for a special event or a fancy-dress party, treat it gently. Try not to handle it too much and be careful with substances like wine and coffee that can easily stain it. Even if it seems in good condition, put it away carefully after use. Keep it in its closed position, making sure the paper or fabric is folded accurately. Wrap it in acid-free tissue (see pages 148-156), clean linen or pure cotton cloth, and try to keep the temperature constant.

If your fan is very fragile, you'll probably have to keep it for display only, but you still need to be careful about the conditions. Avoid direct sunlight, strong artificial lighting and positions close to central heating sources. All these are liable to dry out the fan, so that adhesives may be weakened, the leaf may split or come away from the frame, and the frame may warp. Damp conditions are a problem too, as these can cause brown foxing spots on paper fans, or rusting of metal decoration such as sequins – which will stain and rot a fabric background. To protect the fan and keep it in a stable environment, you could frame it, but it's worth having this done professionally and asking the framer to use museum- or conservation-quality materials.

Left: Bone-handled cutlery is a frequent flea-market find, but check the authenticity of the grain to make sure it isn't cleverly finished plastic.

145

PRACTICAL BASKETWARE

Think laterally and find practical uses for the different shapes and sizes of baskets you come across in markets.

○ Big lidded laundry baskets, sometimes with leather straps to fasten them, provide alternative blanket boxes. Use them to store linens, blankets and curtains and provide bedside tables.

○ Laundry baskets and picnic hampers are also perfect for children's rooms: the lids are so light that there's no risk of children getting trapped inside them or of fingers being crushed. Use them for toys and for woollen clothes such as socks and sweaters.

○ Smaller, open-top baskets provide invaluable storage around the house and garden (look out for bicycle baskets with a flat back, which will sit neatly against a wall). Use baskets in hallways (for scarves, gloves, dog leashes), garden sheds (for tools, twine, seed packets and gardening gloves), in bathrooms and kitchens (for utensils and toiletries) and to hold sewing or knitting paraphernalia.

○ If you find a particularly nice design, fill it with appropriate goodies and turn it into a ready-wrapped present.

---

to clean your baskets

Try dissolving pure sea salt in warm water (about 30g per 600ml) then scrubbing gently with a stiff brush. Rinse thoroughly and leave them to dry naturally in a warm airy place.

Q How can I mend broken cane or wickerwork? And what's the best way of cleaning it?

A Second-hand markets are a good source of basketware and wickerwork of all kinds, but it's often in dubious condition. Cleaning and repainting furniture won't be a problem, but mending breaks or holes is more difficult, so check pieces thoroughly before buying. Be especially careful with lightweight cane-seated chairs. These were popular in the 19th century but were really designed for bedrooms, where they were decorative rather than functional and wouldn't have to withstand much weight. They're perfect for draping clothes over, but not nearly strong enough for regular use around a dining table. This is not just practical advice for taking care of them in future: it's also a good reason to check the soundness of the caning before you buy, to make sure that it hasn't been stretched or weakened by past misuse. Having a chair re-caned tends to be expensive, as the whole seat has to be cut away and re-woven which may not be worthwhile. If you decide to go ahead, bear in mind that the cost is usually calculated by the number of holes in the frame.

Wicker furniture – the sort easily mistaken for Lloyd Loom (see page 137) – is more robust, as the tightly woven wicker tends to hold it all together. However, you need to be reasonably careful how you treat it, in order not to weaken the under-lying frame. This is usually made from willow rods that have a natural polish to their surface, so avoid washing the furniture with hot water or strong household cleaners, which will degrade the surface and permeate the wood. Remove loose dust and dirt with a dry paintbrush, then brush the wicker with warm soapy water. Rinse with clean water (a hose makes this easier) and dry it in a warm airy place. Occasional marks can be wiped off with a damp cloth.

Right: Even lightweight shopping baskets will provide useful storage if hung on a kitchen or utility room wall.

ADDRESSSES

FLEAMARKETS

ALABAMA
Birmingham Fairgrounds Flea Market,
Birmingham Alabama State Fairgrounds, Birmingham. First weekend and preceding Friday of every month and first three weekends and preceding Fridays in December; Fridays 3 to 7pm, Saturdays 9am to 6pm, Sundays 9am to 5pm

World's Longest Yard Sale – 450 miles
Starts in Gadsden and proceeds north through Tennessee and Kentucky. Four days in August, dawn till dusk.
For more information
(256) 549-0351
www.127sale.com

ALASKA
Anchorage Downtown Saturday Market
Jct. 3rd and E Sts. Anchorage. Saturdays mid-May through mid-September, 10am to 6pm.
For more information
(907) 272 5634

ARIZONA
Fairgrounds Antiques Market,
Phoenix Arizona State Fairgrounds, Phoenix. Third weekend of January, May, September, and November; Saturdays, 9am to 5pm, Sundays 10am to 4pm.
For more information
(800) 678-9987
www.jackblack.com

ARKANSAS
Thackerland Flea Market,
666 Hwy. 367 Judsonia.
For more information
(501) 729-3063

CALIFORNIA
Long Beach Outdoor Antique and Collectible Market,
Veteran's Stadium, Long Beach. Third Sunday of the month, 8am to 3pm.
For more information
(323) 655-5703

Rose Bowl Flea Market,
Pasadena Rose Bowl, Pasadena. Second Sunday of the month, 9am to 3pm, early bird 7am.
For more information
(323) 560-7469

Santa Monica Airport Outdoor Antique and Collectible Market,
South side of Santa Monica Airport, Airport Avenue, Santa Monica. Fourth Sunday of every month, and the fifth Sunday if there is one, 8am to 3pm; early-bird 6 to 8am.
For more information
(323) 933-2511

COLORADO
Lafayette Flea Market,
130 E. Spaulding, Lafayette. Every day, 10am to 6pm.
For more information
(303) 665-0433

CONNECTICUT
Farmington Antiques Weekend,
Farmington Polo Grounds, 1-84, exit 39, Farmington. Second weekend in June and Labor Day Weekend, 10am to 5pm, early bird Saturday 7am.
For more information
(317) 598-0019
www.farmington–antiques.com

Elephant's Trunk Bazaar,
Route 7, New Milford. Sundays March through December, 6.45am to 2.30pm.
For more information
(860) 355-1448

Woodbury Antiques and Flea Market,
Main Street, near Jct. Rtes 6 and 64, Woodbury. Saturdays April through November, 5.30am to 1pm.
For more information
(203) 263-2841
www.woodburyfleamarket.com

DELAWARE
New Castle Farmers Market,
Jct. Rte 13 and Hares Corner, New Castle. Friday through Sunday, Fridays and Saturdays year-round 10am to 10pm, Sundays 10am to 6pm.
For more information
(302) 328-4102

FLORIDA
Florida Twin Markets,
Hwy. 441 Mt. Dora. Weekends year-round with three-day extravaganzas in November, January and February, 9am to 5pm.
For more information
(353) 383-8393

Webster Westside Flea Market,
Jct. Hwy. 478 and NW 3rd St. Webster. Mondays year-round, 5am to dusk.
For more information
(800) 832-7396

Piccadilly Antique and Collectible Fair,
South Florida Fairgrounds, West Palm Beach. Usually the first weekend of every month, Saturdays 9am to 5pm, Sundays 10am to 4.30pm, early-bird Fridays 12-5pm.
For more information
(727) 345-4431
www.piccadillypromos.com

GEORGIA

Lakewood Antiques Market,
Lakewood Fairgrounds, Atlanta.
Second weekend and preceding
Friday of every month, Fridays
and Saturdays 9am to 6pm,
Sundays 10am to 5pm, early-
bird Thursdays 3pm.
For more information
(404) 622-4488
www.lakewoodantiques.com

Scotts Antique Market Show,
Atlanta Exposition Center,
Atlanta.
Second weekend and preceding
Friday of every month, Fridays
and Saturdays 9am to 6pm,
Sundays 10am to 4pm.
For more information
(740) 569-4112

HAWAII

**Hawaii All-Collectors Show
and Sale,**
Blaisdell Exhibition Hall,
Honolulu.
Third weekend and preceding
Friday in July; Friday 4 to 9pm,
Saturday 11am to 9pm, Sunday
11am to 5pm.
For more information (808)
941-9754 www.ukulele.com

IDAHO

Cascade Flea Market,
Cascade Airport, Cascade.
Weekends mid-May through
early October, 9am to 6pm.
For more information
(208) 382-3600

ILLINOIS

Third Sunday Market,
McClean County Fairgrounds,
Interstate Center, Bloomington.
Third Sunday of the month
from May through October,
early-bird 6.30am, general
8am to 4pm.
For more information
(800) 433-8226

**First Presbyterian
Rummage Sale,**
First Presbyterian Church, 700
N. Sheridan Road, Lake Forest.
First Thursday in May,
7am to 6pm.
For more information (847)
234-6250

Sandwich Antiques Market,
The Fairgrounds, Sandwich.
Six Sundays a year, in May
through October, 8am to 4pm.
For more information
(773) 227-4464

Kane County Flea Market,
Kane County Fairgrounds.
St Charles. First Sunday and
preceding Saturday of every
month; Saturdays 12 to 5pm,
Sundays 7am to 4pm.
For more information
(630) 377-2252

INDIANA

Barn and Field Flea Market,
Jct. W 151st and Parrish Aves,
Cedarlake.
Weekends year-round, 8am to
4pm.
For more information
(219) 696-7368

**Gray Goose Antiques and
"Collectibles" Fair,**
Franklin Johnson County
Fairgrounds, Franklin.
Various weekends September
through April 9am to 4pm.
For more information
(317) 881-5719

Tri-State Antique Market,
U.S Rte. 50 Lawrenceburg.
First Sunday of the month
from May through October,
7am to 3pm; early bird 6am.
For more information
(513) 738-7256
www.queencityshows.com

IOWA

Midwest Antiques Show,
Hawkeye Downs Fairgrounds,
Cedar Rapids.
First Sunday in April and last
Sunday in October,
9am to 4pm.
For more information
(319) 643-2065

Sharpless Flea Market,
5049 Herbert Hoover Hwy.
NE, exit 249, Iowa City.
Second Sunday of month,
September through May, 8am
to 4pm, early-bird 6am

**Collector's Paradise Flea
Market,**
Keokuk County Fairgrounds,
What Cheer.
First Sunday in May, and
October, 7 am to dusk.
For more information
(641) 634-2109

KANSAS

Mid-American Flea Markets,
Kansas State Fairgrounds,
Hutchinson.
First Sunday of the month,
from October through June,
except February, 9am to 4pm.
For more information
(316) 663-5626.
www.midamericamarkets.com

Sparks Flea Market,
Jct K-7 Hwy and Mission
Road, between Troy and
Highland.
Thursday through Sunday,
three times a year, in May, July,
and September, 7am to 6pm.
For more information
(785) 985-2411

KENTUCKY
Kentucky Flea Market,
Kentucky Fair and Exposition
Center, Louisville.
Various weekends, including
preceding Friday, February
through December; Friday 12
to 7pm; Saturday 10am to 7pm,
Sunday 11am to 5pm.
For more information
(502) 456-2244
www.stewartpromotions.com

LOUISIANA
Jefferson Flea Market,
2134 Airline Dr. Kenner.
Fridays, Saturdays, and Sundays
year-round, 10am to 6pm.
For more information
(504) 461-0128

Community Flea Market,
French Market, 1200 block of
N. Peters St. New Orleans.
Every day, 7am to 7pm.
For more information
(504) 596-3420

MAINE
**Wiscasset Old Jail Outdoor
Antiques Show and Sale,**
Old Jail, Federal Street,
Wiscasset.
Last Saturday of August,
9am to 3pm.
For more information
(207) 284-8657

Montsweag Flea Market,
Route 1, Woolwich.
Wednesdays, Saturdays, and
Sundays May through October,
Fridays as well during the
summer. 6.30am to 3pm.
For more information
(207) 443- 2809

MARYLAND
Bonnie Brae Flea Market,
1301 Pulaski Hwy, Edgewood.
Sundays year-round,
7am to 3pm.
For more information
(410) 679-2210

MASSACHUSETTS
**Charlton Antiques,
Charlton Antique and
Flea Market**
Trolley Crossings, Routes 20
and 315,k Charlton.
Sunday year-round, Saturdays
as well as April through
November, Saturdays 9am to
3pm, Sundays 7am to 4pm.
For more information
(508) 248-5690

Brimfield Antiques Show,
Various locations in and
around Brimfield. Three times
a year, in May, July and
September. Tuesday through to
Sunday.
For more information
(413) 283-2418
www.brimfieldshow.com

MICHIGAN
Ann Arbor Antiques Market,
5055 Ann Arbor Saline Road,
Ann Arbor.
One Sunday a month,
7am to 4pm.
For more information
(850) 984-0122

Centreville Antiques Market,
St Joseph's County
Fairgrounds, Centreville.
Five times a year, May through
October, Sunday 7am to 3pm.
For more information
(773) 227-4464

**Flat Rock Historical Society
Antique and Flea Market,**
Flat Rock Speedway,
Flat Rock.
First Sunday in May and
October, 8am to 5pm.
For more information
(734) 782-5220

MINNESOTA
**Downtown Oronoco Gold
Rush,**
Various sites in downtown
Oronoco.
Third weekend in August,
dawn till dusk.
For more information
(507) 367-4405

MISSISSIPPI
**Fairgrounds Antique
Flea Market,**
900 High St. Jackson,
Weekends year-round,
Saturdays 8am to 5pm, Sundays
10am to 5pm.
For more information
(601) 353-5327

MISSOURI
Big Pevely Flea Market,
8773 Commerical Blvd, Pevely.
Weekends year round,
7am to 5pm.
For more information
(636) 479-5400

NEBRASKA
**Brownville, Nebraska Flea
Market,**
Rte 136, Brownville. Last full
weekend in September,
8am to 5pm.
For more information
(402) 825-6001

NEW HAMPSHIRE
Grandview Flea Market,
Jct. Rts. 28 and 28 Bypass,
Derry. Weekends year-round,
7am to 3.30pm
For more information
(603) 432-2326

**Antiques Week in New
Hampshire,**
Manchester
Various locations in and
around Manchester, one week
in August.
For more information
(845) 876-0616

NEW JERSEY
Atlantique City,
Atlantic City Convention
Center, Atlantic City.
Fourth weekend in March and
third weekend in October,
Saturdays 10am to 8pm.
For more information
(609) 926-1800
www.atlantiquecity.com

Columbus Farmer's Market,
2919 Rte. 206 S, Columbus.
Thursday, Saturday, and Sunday
year-round, dawn to 1.30pm.
For more information
(609) 267-0400

**Lambertville Antiques
Market,**
1864 River Road, Lambertville.
Wednesdays, Saturdays, and
Sundays year round, 6am to
4pm.
For more information
(609) 397-0456

Ocean Grove Flea Market,
Historic Richmond Town,
Staten Island.
First Sunday in June, Sunday
after Labor Day, and first
Sunday in October,
10am to 5pm.
For more information
(718) 351-1611

NEW MEXICO
**New Mexico State Fair Flea
Market,**
New Mexico State Fairgrounds,
Albuquerque.
Weekends year-round, except
during State Fair, 7am to 5pm.
For more information
(505) 265-1791

NEW YORK
**Madison-Bouckville Outdoor
Antiques Show,**
Rte, 20 Bouckville.
Third weekend in August,
early-bird Friday 10am,
Saturday and Sunday
9am to 5pm.
For more information
(315) 824- 2462
www.bouckvilleantiqueshow.com

**The Annex Antiques Fair and
Flea Market,**
6th Avenue between 25th and
26th Streets, New York City.
Weekends year-round, 9am
to 5pm.
For more information
(212) 243-5343

Triple Pier Expo,
Passenger Ship Piers 88, 90,92
New York City.
Two weekends in March and
two weekends in November.
Saturday 9am to 6pm, Sunday
11am to 7pm.
For more information
(212) 255-0020

**Stormville Airport Antique
Show and Flea Market,**
Rte. 216, Stormville.
Weekends of Memorial Day,
Fourth of July, Labor Day and
Columbus Day, last Sunday in
April, and first Sunday in
August and November; dawn
till dusk.
For more information
(845) 221-6561

NORTH CAROLINA
**Metrolina Expo Antiques &
Antique Collectibles Market,**
7100 Statesville Road,
Charlotte.
First weekend and preceding
Friday of every month based
on the first Saturday of the
month, Fridays and Saturdays
8am to 5pm, Sundays 9am to
5pm, early-bird Wednesdays
9am to 5pm. For more
information
(800) 824-3770
www.metrolinaantiqueshow.com

Fairgrounds Flea Market,
North Carolina State
Fairgrounds, Jct. Blue Ridge
Road and Hillsboro St.
Raleigh.
Weekends November through
September, 9am to 5pm.
For more information
(919) 829-3533

NORTH DAKOTA
**Dakota Midwest Flea Market
and Antique Show,**
Mandan Community Center,
901 Division St. Mandan.
First weekend of every month
except January, Saturdays 9am
to 5pm, Sundays 10am to 4pm.
For more information
(701) 852-1289

OHIO
Scott's Antique Market,
Ohio Exposition Center,
Columbus.
One weekend a month from
November through June,
Saturdays 9am to 6pm, Sundays
10am to 4pm

**Springfield Antique Show
and Flea Market,**
Clark County Fairgrounds,
Springfield.
Third weekend and preceding
Friday of every month, Fridays
5 to 8pm, Saturdays 8 am to
5pm, Sundays 9 am to 4pm.
Early-bird Friday before 12pm.
For more information
(937) 325-0053

OKLAHOMA
Mary's Ole Time Swap Meet,
Jct. 23rd St and Midwest Blvd,
Oklahoma City.
Weekends year-round, dawn to
dusk.
For more information
(405) 427-0051

Tulsa Flea Market,
Tulsa Fairgrounds,
 Jct 21 St and Yale, Tulsa.
Saturdays mid-October through
mid-September, 8am to 5pm.
For more information
(918) 744-1386

OREGON
**Catlin Gabel School
Rummage Sale,**
Portland Exposition Center,
Portland.
First weekend and preceding
Thursday and Friday of
November, Thursday 5 to 9pm,
Friday and Saturday 10am to
6pm, Sunday 10am to 3pm.
For more information
(503) 297-1894 ext. 423

PENNSYLVANIA
Renninger's Antiques Market,
Rte 272, Adamstown.
Sundays year-round, 7am
to 4pm.
For more information
(877) 336-2177

Renninger's Antique Market 2,
749 Nobel St. Kutztown.
Saturdays year-round, 8am
to 5pm.
For more information
(610) 683-6848

Collector's Cove,
Jct. Rtes. 33 and 209, Sciota.
Saturdays and Sundays year-
round, 9am to 5pm.
For more information
(570) 992-5110
www.covemarket.com

RHODE ISLAND
General Stanton Flea Market,
4115A Old Post Road,
Charleston.
Weekends April through
November, 7am to 4pm.
For more information
(401) 364-8888

SOUTH CAROLINA
Lowcountry Market, Gaillard
Auditorium,
77 Calhoun St. Charleston.
Usually the third weekend of
every month, Saturdays 9am to
6pm, Sundays 10am to 5pm.
For more information
(843) 849-1949

SOUTH DAKOTA
Sioux Falls Flea Market,
Expo Center, Sioux Falls.
First full weekend of the month
except June, July, and August;
Saturdays 9am to 5pm, Sundays
11am to 4pm.
For more information
(605) 334-1312

TENNESSEE
**Flea Market at the Nashville
Fairgrounds,**
Tennesee State Fairgrounds,
Nashville.
Fourth weekend of every
month except December,
Saturdays 6am to 6pm, Sundays
7 am to 4pm.
For more information
(615) 862 5016

TEXAS
Austin Country Flea Market,
9500 Hwy. 290 Austin.
Weekends year round, 10am
to 6pm.
For more information
(512) 928-2795

First Monday Trade Days,
Hwy. 19. Canton.
Thursday through Sunday
preceding the first Monday of
every month, dawn till dusk.
For more information
(903) 567-6556
www.firstmonday.com

**Antiques Week in Round
Top,**
Round Top
Various locations in and around
Round Top. Twice a year,
Tuesday through Sunday of the
first full week of April and
October. **Round Top Antiques
Fair** Saturday 9am to 6pm,
Sunday 9am to 4pm,
**Marburger Farm Antique
Show** early-bird Tuesday 10am
to 2pm, Wednesday through
Saturday 9am to 5pm.
For more information
(281) 493-5501
www.roundtopantiquesfair.com;
**Marburger Farm Antique
Show** (800) 947-5799
www.roundtop-marburger.com

VERMONT
Charlotte Flea Market,
Route 7, Charlotte.
Weekends April through
November, 6am to 5pm.
For more information
(802) 425-2844.

Manchester Flea Market,
Jct. Rtes. 11 and 30 Manchester
Center.
Weekends through October,
6am to 5pm.
For more information
(802) 362 1631

**Wilmington Outdoor
Antique and Flea Market**,
Jct. Rtes. 9 and 100,
Wilmington.
Weekends and holiday
Mondays, Memorial Day
through weekend after
Columbus Day, dawn to dusk.
For more information
(802) 464-3345

VIRGINIA
Manor Mart Flea Market,
Hwy. 1 Fredericksburg,
Weekends year-round, dawn
to dusk.
For more information
(540) 898-4685

Richmond Big Flea,
Richmond Raceway Complex,
600 E Laburnum Avenue,
Richmond.
Various weekends year round,
Saturdays 10am to 6pm,
Sundays 12 to 5pm.
For more information
(757) 430-4735
www.bigfleamarket.com

WASHINGTON
Fremont Sunday Market,
Jct. N. 34th St and Fremont
Ave. Seattle.
Sundays May through October,
10am to 5pm.
For more information
(206) 781-6776

**Lakeside School
Rummage Sale**,
Stadium Exhibition Center
between Seahawks Stadium and
Safeco Field, Seattle.
Usually the first weekend and
preceding Friday in March,
Friday and Saturday 10am to
6pm, Sunday 10am to 2pm.
For more information
(206) 440-2740
www.lakesideschool.org

WASHINGTON D.C
Capitol Hill Flea Market
Hine Junior High School
across from the historic Eastern
Market.
Saturdays, best buys before
10am.
www.capitolhillfleamarket.com

WEST VIRGINIA
Harpers Ferry Flea Market,
Jct Hwy 340 and
Bloomery Road,
Harpers Ferry.
Weekends March through
November, dawn till dusk.
For more information
(304) 725-4141
www.harpersferryfleamkt.com

WISCONSIN
Adams Flea Market,
55 S. Main St. Adams.
Weekends year-round, Fourth
of July, and holiday Mondays
May through October, 6am
to 4pm.
For more information
(608) 339-5651

Princeton Flea Market,
Princeton City Park,
Princeton.
Saturdays April through
October 6am to 2pm.
For more information
(920) 295-3877

WYOMING
Antique Show and Sale,
Central Wyoming Fairgrounds,
Casper.
First full weekend in June and
October, Saturdays 10am to
5pm, Sundays 10am to 4pm.
For more information
(307) 234-6663

CANADA

ALBERTA
**Calgary Summer Antiques
Fair**,
Canada Olympic Park, Calgary.
One weekend a year, in late
June or early July, Saturday 9am
to 5pm, Sunday 10am
to 5pm.
For more information
(800) 667-0619

**Hillhurst-Sunnyside
Community Center Flea
Market**,
1320 5th Ave. SE, Calgary.
Weekends year-round, 9am
to 5pm.
For more information
(403) 291-5208

BRITISH COLUMBIA
**Best of the West Antique
Expo**,
Tradex Exhibition Centre,
Abbotsford.
Two weekends a year, in July
and November, Saturdays 9am
to 5pm, Sundays 10am to 5pm.
For more information
(800) 667-0619

Vancouver Flea Market,
703 Terminal Ave, Vancouver.
Weekends year-round, 9am
to 5pm.
For more information
(604) 685-0666

NEW BRUNSWICK
NBAAC Flea Market
Princess Louise Park, Sussex.
One Friday through Sunday in
August, 8am to 8pm.
For more information
(506) 684-4394

NOVA SCOTIA

Windsor Country Fair Flea Market,
Hwy. 101 Windsor.
Weekends mid-June through early September, 9.30am to 4.30pm.
For more information
(902) 798-0000

ONTARIO

Christie Classic Antique Show,
Christie Conservation Area, Dundas.
Two Saturdays a year, May and September, 8am to 5pm.
For more information
(888) 594-9297

Aberfoyle Antique Market,
RR 3, Guelph.
Sundays late April through late October, 8am to 4pm.
For more information
(519) 763-1077

Sunday Antiques Market,
Market Square behind City Hall, Kingston.
Sundays May through October, dawn till dusk.
For more information
(613) 544-2495

Stouffville Country Market,
12555 Tenth Line N., Stouffville.
Weekends year-round, Saturdays 8am to 4pm, Sundays 9am to 4pm.
For more information
(905) 640-3813

Toronto Sunday Market,
92 Front St. E, Toronto.
Sundays year-round, dawn till dusk.
For more information
(416) 410-1310

PRINCE EDWARD ISLAND

70 mile Coastal Yard Sale,
Sites along and around Rte. 1, Charlottetown.
One weekend a year in mid- to late September, dawn till dusk.
For more information
(888) 734-7529

QUEBEC

Marché aux Puces de Cinq Etoiles,
Exit 78 off Autoroute 10, Bromont.
Sundays early May late October, 7am to 5pm.
For more information
(514) 875-5500

USEFUL REFERENCE

Stone
National Stone Association,
2101 Wilson Blvd., Ste.100, Arlington Virginia, 22201
Tel: 703 525-8788
Fax: 703 525-7782
www.gemsrocks.com
Worldwide information trading site to promote trade in minerals & mineral products.

Old School Stone Restoration,
Newburgh, NY 12550
(845) 565-9335

Golberg Restoration Company,
411 Westmount Drive
Los Angeles, CA 90048
(310) 652-0735
Provides stone restoration services including marble, sandstone, bone and other natural stones.
www.restorationworld.com

Glass
The Glass Art Society
A professional organisation whose purpose is to support and encourage excellence, to advance education and to promote the appreciation and development of the glass arts.
www.glassart.org

The National Glass Association–
8200 Greensboro Dr, Ste 302, McLean Virginia, 22102.
Tel: (703) 442-4890
Fax: (703) 442-0630
www.glass.org
Provides information, education, related business services and a forum for education and ideas exchange.

Society of Glass & Ceramic Decorators,
4340 East-West Highway, Suite 200,
Bethesda Maryland, 20814.
Tel: (301) 951-3933
www.sgcd.org

Broken Art Restoration,
Chicago, IL.
(815) 472-3900

Glass Restoration,
New York, NY.
(212) 517-3287

Collectors Sales and Services
www.antiqueglass.com
For Early American Glass and Staffordshire.

Jewellery
www.beadsearch.com
Provides links, free classes and advice, galleries, information sites, clubs for those who love beads.

www.stephaniebesco.com
Handmade glass bead website.

www.watchus.com
Website offering links and information about gems, charms both silver and gold, buttons, beads, chains, watches, diamonds, glass, wood, polymer clay and wire jewellery.

The National Bead Society
Dedicated to the academic study of beads and dissemination of bead information.
www.nationalbeadsociety.com

The International Society of Glass Beadmakers
Non-profit organization dedicated to promoting and supporting the art of making hand-crafted glass beads.
www.sgb.org

Ceramics & Metalware
www.ceramicsworldauction.com
Website listing names and addresses of ceramic and craft associations.

www.claystation.com
Provides listings of societies, councils, travel, exhibitions, conferences and workshops relating to clay.

American Ceramic Society,
P.O. Box 6136, Westerville, Ohio. 43086-6136
Tel: (614) 890-4700
Fax: (614) 899-6109
Leading organization dedicated to the advancement of ceramics. It can provide the latest technical, scientific and educational information to meet the needs of the ceramics community, related fields, and the general public.

www.tias.com
Website with useful suggestions and contacts for fine antiques and collectibles.

ClayNet International
http://home.vicnet.net.au/~claynet/claynet.htm
Non-profit forum for international ceramic art on the web. Provides listings of educational institutes, galleries, museums, forums, bookshops and commercial sites.

Textiles
www.sallyqueenassociates.com
Website offering advice on preservation and care of costumes and textiles

The Costume Society of America,
55 Edgewater Drive, PO Box 73, Earleville, MD, 21919
www.costumesocietyamerica.com

www.conservationresources.com
Website offering advice on restoration and preservation, plus information on auctions, dealer's antique and vintage, historical societies and museums.

www.costumegallery.com
Website offering information and products related to textiles, see www.textilefabric.com for textile fabric consultants. Or see www.antique-fashion.com for Karen Augusta, an antique and lace specialist.

www.handmaderugs.com
Company based in San Francisco that specializes in rug dealing, preservation, conservation.

University of Nebraka. International Quilt Study Centre.
www.quiltstudy.unl.edu

International Quilt Association
Parent organization of shows International Quilt festival, International Quilt market, Patchwork and Quilt expo
www.quilts.com

Alicia Repairs Textiles,
New Orleans, LA.
(504) 862 9956 (restorers)

Rocky Mountain Quilts,
York Village, ME;
(800) 762-5940 (restorers)
www.rockymountainquilts.com

Leather
www.leatherique.com
Website that provides products to help restore and preserve leather.

Paintings, Prints and Paper
Antiquarian Bookseller's Association
Provides millions of rare, used, and out-of-print books.
www.bibliofind.com

Appelbaum and Himmelstein,
New York, NY;
(212) 666-4630 (restorers)

Picture Restoration Studio, Inc.
San Francisco, CA
(415) 648-4781

www.1art.com
Website with a forum for discussion and advice on restoring and preserving, paintings, paper and prints.

155

www.philatelics.com
Stamp collector's website.

www.stampfinder.com
Offers global stamp exchange,
sale.

www.eclipsepaper.com
Professional paper conservation
website.

Heirloom Art Studio,
2616 Wears Valley Road,
Sevierville, Tennessee,
37862-8300
Tel: (865) 428-4900
Gives advice on photography,
fine art restoration
www.heirloomartstudio.com

Furniture
www.oakplus.com
Website that lists useful
contacts for furniture, for
instance the Furniture History
Society.

www.furnitureguide.com
Has a link to useful furniture
repair and maintenance,
markets and library contacts.

Furniture Medic,
www.furnituremedic.com
U.S nationwide furniture
restoration company.

**Fran's Wicker & Rattan
Furniture,**
www.franswicker.com
Website for America's oldest
and largest importers of wicker
and rattan furniture.

Furniture Medic
Nationwide furniture
restoration company.
www.furnituremedic.com

The Furniture Wizard,
www.furniturewizard.com
Website that provides a wealth
of information about the
restoration of antiques,
furniture repair and refinishing.
Plus cutting edge information
and techniques as they emerge
in the industry.

**American Furniture
Manufacturers Association**
PO Box HP-7 High Point,
North Carolina 27261;
Tel: (336) 884-5000
www.afma4u.org
Website provides names of
suppliers and manufacturers of
home furnishings within all
states. Information on resources
and industry.

www.iserv.net
Website listing furniture and
design associations world-wide.

Woodworkers Directory
www.woodindustry.com
An easy-to-use, searchable
database of architectural
woodworkers, cabinet
designers, furniture makers,
musical instrument builders,
picture framers, wood finishers.

The Furniture Society –
Box 18, Free Union, VA 22940
www.furnituresociety.org
mail@furnituresociety.org
Tel: (434) 973-1488
fax: (434) 973-0336

Specialists
**American Horticultural
Society**
www.ahs.org

Antique Collectors Club
www.antiquecc.com
Publishers of monthly antiques
magazine *Antique Collecting*
which caters for collectors
interested in widening their
knowledge of antiques

The Online Collector
www.theonlinecollector.com

Conservation advice and materials
**American Institute of
Conservation (AIC),**
1717 K Street, Suite 301,
Washington D.C 2006
Tel: (202) 452-9545

www.antiquerestorers.com
Website listing over 500 antique
restorers throughout U.S.

www.antiqueresources.com
Website offering email feedback
from an 'antique doctor' who
can help you with any questions
you may have.

**The Antique Restorers
Association**
www.assoc-restorers.com

www.pages.tias.com
Kovals online directory of
restorators and conservators.

**North West Arts Objects
Conservation:**
Art and antique repair and
restoration: porcelain, ceramics,
wood, stone, painting, metal,
ivory, paper, fabric, books,
gilding, leather, and more
www.nwartsource.com
Email:
restore@nwartsource.com
Tel: (503) 288-8414

Golberg Restoration
Company:
411 Westmount Drive
Los Angeles, CA 90048
(310) 652-0735
Restoration services in stone,
painting, furniture, and
porcelain.

Fleamarket and Antique Fairs
www.wholesalebuyersguide.
com

www.ukulele.com
Antiques website for collectors
of jewellery, prints, wooden and
metal antiques, restorers, even
an antiques 'wanted pin board'
section

www.fleamarketguide.com
Click a state to find listings of
fleemarkets throughout U.S.

www.antiqueshowscanada.com
Listings of antique shows
throughout US.

**www.woodworkersauction.
com**
Lists of flea markets, antique
shows, collectibles, crafters,
promoters and vendors for
street fairs and festivals.

Auctions and Trade Shows
Christie's
International auctioneer of fine
art and collectibles
www.christies.com

Sotheby's
www.sothebys.com
Online auctions of fine arts,
antiques and collectibles.

www.tsnn.com
Online source for trade shows
and conference information.

PHOTOGRAPHIC ACKNOWLEDGMENTS

Caroline Arber   2, 6, 17, 22, 26, 42, 80, 111

Jan Baldwin   75

Charles Colmer   24, 71, 140

Christopher Drake   10, 65, 91, 115, 121, 124

Craig Fordham   69

Kate Gadsby   9, 35, 100

Catherine Gratwicke   50, 67

Huntley Hedworth   79, 85, 136

Tom Leighton   5, 15, 21, 39, 103, 147

Simon McBride   94

James Merrell   18, 82, 96, 130

Diana Miller   116

Andrew Montgomery   41, 55, 127

Tham Nhu Tran   33, 107

Bridget Peirson   31, 108

Alex Ramsay   62, 142

Pippa Rimmer   1

Bob Smith   87, 88

Debi Treloar   47, 52

Pia Tryde   49, 58, 77, 99, 123, 128, 139, 144

Polly Wreford   56, 112

Styling by Hester Page, Ben Kendrick, Sophie
Martell, Laura Vine, Kristin Peters and
Pippa Rimmer.